Strength from within

SA'DIYYA NESAR

Strength from Within: Personal insight on how to cope, grow and flourish during life's trials on my life with physical disabilities

First Published in England by
Kube Publishing Ltd
MCC, Ratby Lane, Markfield,
Leicestershire, UK
Tel: +44 (0) 1530 249230
E-Mail: info@kubepublishing.com
Website: www.kubepublishing.com

Author: Sa'diyya Nesar
Editor: Umm Marwan Ibrahim
Cover Design: Afreen Fazil (Jaryah Studios)
Typesetting: LiteBook Prepress Services

A Cataloguing-in-Publication Data record for this book is
available from the British Library.

ISBN 978-1-84774-223-0 Paperback
ISBN 978-1-84774-224-7 Ebook

Printed in Turkey by Elma Basim

"As a disability rights activist and disabled Muslim woman, I wanted to vicariously experience another woman's disability journey of trials and triumphs with whom I share some of my intersectional identities including faith and ethnicity. Sa'diyya articulates and correlates faith in deep and meaningful ways to reconcile the questions before her in order to develop her resilience. Her spiritual reflections about verses from the Holy Qur'an, Prophetic sayings and stories of the prophets who had disabilities in their lives deepens the reader's understanding of how a Muslim should view disablement whether they have their own lived experience or not. This book is a must read because Sa'diyya does an incredible job of enlightening the reader and capturing their attention with her words and wisdom, describing significant moments in her life, and how she resolves them with her faith, dispelling any myths and fears that one may have about living with a disability." *Rabia Khedr, CEO of DEEN Support Services and Founder of Muslims With Disabilities International, is a married mother of four adults and is blind.*

"Masha Allah, brilliantly written! 'Strength from Within' is a profound testament to resilience and spiritual fortitude, offering personal insights on navigating life's trials from an Islamic perspective, particularly for those with physical disabilities. As a reader with lived experience of physical disability, I resonated deeply with Sa'diyya's journey, finding solace in her acceptance of Allah's decree. The book compellingly redirects focus toward endurance, growth, and seizing the best from challenging situations, making it a highly spiritual and relatable read." *Rafia Haniff-Cleofas, Life coach, Disability Advocate, Founder of Muslims with Disabilities International*

"*Strength from within*," is a survival manual, not only for people with disabilities, but every human who needs inspiration. Sa'diyya's journey parallels with her sincere faith in the Almighty. Each chapter beautifully follows her spiritual growth and strength. Sa'diyya shares her beautiful life story while referencing the endurance of Allah's Prophets. The book is an intricately woven tapestry of unwavering faith, beautiful patience and awe-inspiring resilience from this remarkable writer." *Tasnim Jadwat, Mum of Iman, Spinal Muscular Atrophy warrior, Master Chef South Africa*

This book is dedicated to all parents of children with disabilities. I especially dedicate it to my parents, in particular, my mother. May the Almighty always be pleased with you for giving up your Ph.D. in dedication to my growth.

Āmīn.

Contents

Acknowledgements

I firstly thank Allah ﷻ for giving me the chance to write and complete this book. It is through His mercy and the people that He has sent in my life that this completion is a reality.

I thank my parents for providing the best education and resources for me to learn, grow, and accomplish. The guiding support from both my father and mother has been a source of strength. I am grateful to my grandparents—especially my Na Na Jee—for teaching me what life has to offer no matter how grim the circumstances.

May Allah ﷻ honour all of you and all your descendants for providing the best environment at home for me to grow.

I am grateful to my husband—my supporting friend—for helping me write some of the most difficult memories in my life. You are Allah's mercy upon me, and I pray that Allah ﷻ always chooses you amongst those He holds dear.

I thank both of my younger brothers—my first true friends. Both of you have always been the wind beneath my wings.

I thank Ilhaam, Imogen, Samiha, and Sarah for redirecting me to complete this book and being true sister-friends.

I thank Mrs. Alexander and Mrs. Merritt for teaching me to read and write—thank you for showing me that teachers can also be your friends.

I thank Uncle Aziz and his family for visiting me at the hospital with a book on the stories of the Prophets—I held every word dear.

I thank Uncle Jalal and his family for believing in me and my studies—your sincerity is what strengthened me to keep going.

I thank Aunty Ayesha for taking care of me as her own daughter so that I could reach my goals. I thank Imam Sulaiman and his family for teaching me like their own. I thank Aunty Atiya as the first author to guide me. I thank everyone from the SISTERs magazine family for including me as your writer sister, and I give special thanks to Reyhana Sidat Ismail for designing my original book cover.

I thank Kube Publishing for believing in me & supporting this book, and give special thanks to Kube's editor Umm Marwan Ibrahim with the final stage. I mostly thank my dearest book coaches—Hend Hagazi and Na'ima B Robert—for strengthening and guiding me throughout the whole writing, editing, and book journey process.

May every word written weigh heavily on all of your scales and may it be a means for all the Prophets to greet all of you with joy.

Āmīn.

Foreword

I first 'met' Sa'diyya Nesar many years ago when we were both writers for Sisters Magazine – a magazine written by Muslim women for Muslim women. Over the years we have touched base a number of times where we have discussed our published books, Sa'diyya's advocacy for individuals with disabilities and my work for the charity I founded that supports revert women in difficulty. There have been many times that we have discussed part of her mission which overlaps with my own in the work that I do: that Muslims, especially reverts with disabilities who are marginalised twice, find the support they need. In her own words that she recently shared with me: 'Revert care needs to be understood and developed within the disability space, and disability care needs to be understood and developed within the general revert care space. This gap needs to be bridged with Allah swt's help and mercy.' Reading this book has made me realise how truly important it is for disability care to be understood and developed in all spaces.

When Sa'diyya approached me to read her book, 'Strength From Within' - a book that includes her personal insights about how to grow in faith while living with a disability, I knew writing this foreword would be an honour.

However, it was only when I began to read it and enter into Sa'diyya's world - both as little Sa'diyya and as adult Sa'diyya, that I realised what a true gift this book is to the reader and indeed the world – whether you have a disability or not.

Reading 'Strength From Within' took me back in time to meeting Muslim men and women who were born with, or later developed disabilities. On each occasion, I would wonder at the strength my brothers and sisters possessed in journeying through this dunya with such trials. My focus was always upon their physical disabilities that produced challenges for what is easy for so many of us. However, reading Sa'diyya's book changed something within me. Though these disabilities have produced difficulties and trials the non-disabled of us will never be able to fathom, there is a strength; a power that Allah azza wa jal develops and nurtures within all those who are tested in this way. And this comes across ever so strongly in this book. So much so, that not only did I enter a world that is unknown and unfamiliar to me, and learned from it, but I too became strengthened through its messages, lessons and invitations to reflect and grow. I can only imagine, if this was the result of reading this book, pausing regularly to absorb its faith-based lessons - looking out of the window and reflecting on my own life, without a disability; I can only imagine the support, comfort and direction that will be taken by Muslim readers with disabilities as well as family and caregivers who support them.

All marginalised groups must be given a voice. I advocate for this strongly in all that I do. But with stereotypes that unfortunately still exist today surrounding disability, I feel Sa'diyya's voice, especially in this book is crucial. As a Muslim woman who has since childhood, lived with a disability and has broken through barriers, she not only shines light on the fact that the Muslim community has not developed enough support for Muslims with disabilities and needs to, but also has shown through her own life's example that accepting Allah's Decree and journeying through the challenges of disability with true emaan can open up doors and possibilities both spiritually and externally in the world.

This isn't just a personal story of triumph against the odds. This is an invitation to change: for the non-disabled creators and leaders in the Muslim community to step up their understanding, development and support. And it is also a personal invitation to those with a disability to find strength in self, faith and ultimately one's relationship with Allah subhanahu wa ta'ala to find and fulfill their individual purpose, not in spite of a disability, but with it.

There is something that made me smile as I read 'Strength From Within'. When Sa'diyya was a little girl, she was given books by her parents which became her companions during her times spent in hospital. Many of these books were about the stories of the prophets and she refers to these stories with their deeper meanings and lessons throughout this book. Connected to this, is my personal reason why I feel everyone should read this book and care about its message. All Prophets came with a message to direct humankind to worship one Creator alone. They took people away from darkness and guided them towards light. They provided us with a blueprint in how to navigate our imperfections by focusing our hearts and souls upon The One who is Perfect. We are all imperfect, regardless of having a disability or not. Our imperfections are there to remind us of our purpose for the sake of the One who possesses none. This book removes the reader from the darkness of ignorance surrounding disability and towards the light of understanding, hope and change for all. For an author to achieve this with a book written about a niche topic points to the strength she has found within her disability and within her faith. Get ready to have your own faith and possibilities transformed.

Aliyah Umm Raiyaan,

Sunday Times Bestselling author of '*Ramadan Reflections*', and '*The Power of Du'a*', founder and CEO of Registered Charity Solace UK for revert women in difficulty.

Preface

Strength from Within[1] is a promise that I made to Allah[2] ﷻ as an eight-year-old girl trapped in the hospital for four months.

I was admitted to the hospital for pneumonia, but it was not pneumonia alone that alarmed the doctors. I could not cough properly since my muscles were weak. My inability to breathe or cough properly was due to muscular weaknesses. I was diagnosed with muscular myopathy as a baby. I was never able to crawl, but later could walk slowly. I could barely climb stairs, then was not able to at all. I just about managed to get up from my chair or change until, eventually, I needed full assistance. I was at high risk of having ordinary cases of flu turn into pneumonia.

---

1 'Strength from Within' was completed in early 2020 so it was written prior to the pandemic. The book announced towards the end of this book will contain more pandemic based disability experiences, God willing.

2 'Allah' is the Arabic word for the monotheistic God recognized in Judaism, Christianity, and Islam.

During the period I had pneumonia at eight years of age, my inability to cough caused build-up within my lungs. The more build-up I had, the more difficult it was to breathe. Eventually, one of my lungs collapsed, and I had to be ventilated in the ICU. The tube was ultimately removed, but the function of my lungs never truly recovered. I ended up needing to use a breathing machine whenever I lay down, and I still do to this day.

Eventually, I was released from the ICU and moved to a private room due to the fear that I might retract viruses from other children. I had to regain my physical strength since I had spent almost a month lying down. I was eventually well enough to read books and have hospital tutors visit for studies. I felt energized and did not understand why I was still prevented from leaving the hospital. Doctors visited every morning, but they withdrew shortly, every time leaving me to think I would be released the next day. This routine went on for weeks until I eventually lost hope.

I retreated into the books that I received from my parents. The books given to me were mostly on the stories of the Prophets[3], and how they endured and overcame difficulties as well as isolation. One thing was consistent amongst all these Prophets: their prayers to Allah ﷻ amidst their trials. Despite their adversities, they had the strength from within them to not only remain patient, but to also do good.

---

3   The stories of the Prophets are from the Abrahamic religions Judaism, Christianity, and Islam. This book accounts for stories of the Prophets from authentic Islamic tradition due to my personal upbringing as a Muslim. This book is intended to be a safe space for all readers interested in learning about the intersection of Disability and Islam.

I could see how their examples could be a guide to how to cope with my own difficulty and remain strong when my parents had to leave after visiting hours. Prophets faced fears, and how they responded to their fears could direct me on how to respond to mine whenever it felt like my health—and my life—was out of control. The awareness that Prophets were able to be patient with gratitude despite their difficulties provided hope, that I could acquire patience, regardless of how long I had to stay in the hospital.

I could see the strength found within the Prophets, but I did not know how to apply it to my own life. We know of the challenges the Prophets faced and are told how they coped, but we get confused when it comes to relating these stories to our own lives. We wonder how to keep standing and not crumble despite the difficulties. We do not understand the whys of our trials, and we are unable to find a way out. We pray, plead, and make promises to Allah ﷻ, begging Him to help us get out of our difficulty.

As that little eight-year-old girl, I wanted to get out of my trial.

When the doctor came in one morning for his regular check-up, I noticed that he stayed longer than usual. He scratched his head, flicked through the files, left the room, and returned to skim through the data again. The slight change in routine gave me a glimmer of hope, that there was a possible chance for me to be released soon, but what he said crushed me:

'It looks like you have to stay for at least another month.'

My heart dropped.

Four months had already passed, and now the doctor was telling me I would have to remain for another month! I grew tired of finding nothing but disappointment from doctors, so I quickly turned to Allah ﷻ after my mother's guidance once the doctor left. I was now expecting things only from Allah ﷻ, especially after reading about His Prophets. I asked Him to release me. I prayed that He would forgive me and help me not complain. I asked that He would teach me what patience is and help me find strength from within. I told Him to not let me stay for another week, let alone another month. I promised that I would do good, especially if it meant that I would be discharged from the hospital soon. I expressed that I would comfort others going through difficulties and share whatever I learn from the lives of the Prophets, my life, and the world around me. I promised that I would write a book one day to uplift others just as the books I had read helped me cope with my trials. I would do all that if it meant that Allah ﷻ kept me alive and set me free to go back home within the week.

The next morning, the doctor came into my room and took even longer than the morning before. He seemed puzzled and confused, saying he would consult with another paediatrician. I did not expect anything and instead busied myself with reading books and talking to my mother. The doctor arrived with the paediatrician to discuss my medical file. A few minutes later, one of the doctors said the five words that I would never forget.

'You can go home soon.'

To my surprise, I was discharged within the week. The hospital that had once trapped me was now a place of endless possibilities, due to the power of prayer. To witness my prayer answered freed me to realize that our hardships are temporary, and that I should have been patient, especially since the time spent there was for a reason and purpose. My time there was not only to recover, but to better understand the realities of life. I may have been going through the same routine within a confined room every day, but there was something to learn, especially if I just opened myself to my circumstances. There was always something to discover and appreciate. Being discharged from the hospital was the start of understanding the importance of prayers amidst hardships. It was the beginning of learning what patience and gratitude meant. My release was the first step in having hope in Allah ﷻ. It was the first impetus to further dig into the stories of the Prophets to understand how they coped and mustered that strength from within, despite their difficulties. It was the first sign that I must fulfill my promise and share whatever I learned.

So, this book is the fulfillment of my promise to Allah ﷻ, the One that heard, answered, and released that eight-year-old girl from the hospital. It contains the most challenging encounters from my life with physical disabilities. It delves into the struggles that I faced both externally and internally, and how I coped. It delves into the reality of how we all face adversities and the beauty that can be found within these hardships. It uncovers lessons that will allow us to appreciate life on a whole different level. This book contains the hidden gems and treasures unearthed from the trials in our lives. The attainment of these treasures may be painful, but it ultimately provides comfort and hope. It allows us to discover strengths that we never thought we had, and to eventually have a more enriched experience. It is a source of encouragement to remain hopeful. It is a reminder to never give up, just like the chosen examples before us.

This book is not a self-help book, nor a memoir, but instead contains personal insights based on what I learned throughout my experiences. Questions posed on social media platforms by the public for the past six years on my work as an international writer and speaker contributed to shaping the content of this book. I have been consulted on a range of topics such as dealing with loss, shame, self-doubt, anxiety, depression, addiction, isolation, discrimination, bullying, dealing with marriage, and recovering from trauma. These questions came not only from those going through such difficulties but also from those witnessing loved ones endure them. I attempt to share my experiences in a way to provide direction, comfort, and hope—the hope to grow and flourish from our adversities instead of letting them bury or drown us.

I hope that this book will bring reassurance and benefit to every single person that reads it. I humbly ask readers from all backgrounds to pray that Allah ﷻ accepts the fulfillment of my promise.

Āmīn.

Chapter 1

Trials in Life—A Seed Preparing to Sprout

Life's Reality

*'We have certainly created **man into hardship.***'
(*al-Balad* 90: 4)

Hardship was a constant reality early on in my childhood. Everyday tasks were hard to manage due to my muscular weaknesses. The struggle in doing everyday tasks was my norm, so it was easy to accept that life is difficult. A lot of peers and adults pitied me for the struggles that I faced. They went as far as apologizing, as if I had been greatly wronged. They indicated that I should not have to live this way, because life—especially for a child—should not be difficult.

The sympathies throughout my early childhood gradually shifted my perception of the world. They caused me to question why life had to be filled with challenges or why I had to face them. I transformed from someone that considered difficulties normal—and very much part of life—to someone that grew troubled over my circumstances. The focus became not on trying to cope, but rather on why I had not been spared, especially as a child. This shift was shown by my increasing inquisitiveness: I asked my parents why I had to face difficulties. I questioned them about Allah 🕮 and why He allowed pain and hardships to occur. My questions were an indication that I did not want to struggle when doing everyday tasks. It was a testament to how I was finding it hard to accept the reality that I was facing. It was a form of denial because I was not questioning with the purpose of understanding; I was questioning as a way of rejecting. It was a means to delay facing and accepting the reality of my life.

We all must one day face the fact that we can never be immune from struggles, because not accepting this truth is living a life of denial. This denial prevents us from learning how to live with our hardships and from making the best of our circumstances. Denial limits us because by not accepting, we put ourselves in a bubble that will eventually pop, causing us to panic.

Everyone will undergo hardships, whether physical, emotional, economic, or spiritual. Some may suffer from losing a child or their health. Others may endure conflicts within the family or strains at work. These are situations many of us are bound to face. Acknowledging these hardships, however, gives us the chance to learn how to better cope and endure.

Difficulties in life exist mostly because this world—unlike Paradise—is one where struggling is required. We will not only taste joy but also sadness, relief along with pain, ease with hardship.

Allah 🙏 says,

> 'And We will surely **test you** with **something of fear**, hunger, loss of wealth, lives, and fruits; but give **good tidings to the patient**.'
> (al-Baqarah 2: 155)

Tests are part of this life. However, the acceptance of this reality will not save us from experiencing fear. We will feel scared because it is our innate instinct to want to escape any difficulty. We all prefer to return to our life of happiness with our health regained. We all want the loved one that we lost returned to us. The experience of deprivation may lead us to feel trapped.

This entrapment can cause us to feel buried in helplessness, able to see nothing but darkness. We may fall into grief and despair. In this state, we are just like seeds that are buried beneath the ground, unable to see the light. A seed that is put under so much pressure that it ultimately cracks.

Trial's Reality

Seeds crack to grow, just as the purpose of life's trials is for us to grow. We may not see it at first, but with time and proper cultivation, we can witness the change. Change cannot occur if we do not accept both the reality of life and the existence of trials. Denial makes us consumed with how to get out, but acceptance gives us the chance to discover the strength from within to sprout. It allows us to shift our focus towards endurance, growth, and making the best out of the situation.

There is an ultimate purpose for being put under pressure and darkness: attaining rewards. Part of this reward may be achieved in this life by noticing life's blessings and learning from our experiences. Trials, therefore, distinguish those who are sincere towards growth from those who complain out of ingratitude and disbelief.

As Prophet Muhammad ﷺ described in a hadith,

> 'A *believer* is like a stalk where the **wind constantly shakes it.** The believer is constantly struck by misfortunes. A **hypocrite** is like a cedar tree [seeming to stand firm], but **once it is shaken, it is rooted out** [not to rise again].' (Muslim)[1]

Cracked Seed to Bloomed Flower

Seeds ultimately sprout from darkness into light through the absorption of water and minerals. The water and minerals that nourished me were the lessons from Islamic figures of the past, especially Prophets, and how they coped with trials.

Allah ﷻ says,

> 'We relate to you of these **stories of the messengers** so that We make _firm your heart_. And there has come to you, in this, the truth, **instruction**, and a **reminder for the believers.**'
>
> (Hūd 11: 120)

Prophets withstood the strongest of winds to be examples for us to learn from, so that we may also know *how* to withstand life's trials and bloom.

---

1 (Ṣaḥīḥ Muslim, 58)

My Trial

It was through reading the stories of the Prophets at the hospital that I got to see how their trials were relatable to my life with physical disabilities. Some of them were, like me, tested with health and disabilities, like Prophets Ayyūb ﷺ, Yaʿqūb ﷺ, and Mūsā ﷺ. I learned through their examples that difficulties are temporary. That in itself comforted me. Then, I started to ask questions about the lives of the Prophets, not for the sake of questioning the decree of Allah ﷻ, but for the sake of understanding my purpose.

Their stories taught me several valuable lessons:

I may have had ill-health, but that does not mean that I would remain ill. We may, at one point, lose something, but that does not imply whatever was lost will never be found. We may feel pressured, but that does not mean relief will not follow. We may feel trapped, but that is not to say we will never break free.

Our trial is not our eternal fate.

Our reward—fruits of growth—is our eternal fate.

My life with disabilities previously put me in a state of darkness where I could not see any hope or reason behind my circumstances. I was so focused on getting out of my difficulty and not wanting to accept my fate. This attitude prevented me from learning from the trial—it hindered my growth.

Learning how the Prophets dealt with difficulties helped me change my outlook despite still living with physical disabilities. I started to believe that whatever I was going through was decreed for a reason. This allowed me to focus on what I could learn and value from the trial, the gains instead of the losses. This mindset led to growth.

Like a seed beneath the ground, my focus was on how to endure and strive to reach my potential.

Like seeds, we are bound to this Earth where we cannot escape. We can either dwell with complaints about why life's trials cracked us open, or we can absorb the lessons from it and sprout.

Chapter 2

The Process of Accepting Life's Trials

We wail the moment we are out of our mothers' wombs because we want to go back to that place of familiarity. As newborns, we eventually adapt to this new world, but we cry the second we are distressed. It might be when we are hungry, cold, or placed in unfamiliar arms. We shed tears not only to seek our mothers' attention but to snatch it fast. The longer it takes, the louder the sobs become, unrelenting until we are returned back to that feeling of comfort.

As adults, we may not automatically cry the second we are distressed, but we still feel uncomfortable in places that are new and unknown. It is a struggle to adapt, and we may break down when overwhelmed. It is natural to want to get out of the difficulty fast. The longer it takes, the more uneasy we feel.

Life requires us to face hardships, overcome them, and grow. We have no choice but to go through this routine simply because we were born. It is easy to say that life's trials are there to help us grow, but it is hard to let the knowledge of this reality guide us to how we should *feel*.

Allah ﷻ says,

> '...mankind was **created weak**.' (*al-Nisā'* 4: 28)
> and,
> 'Man is **created of haste**.' (*al-Anbiyā'* 21: 37)

The haste to return to a place of comfort without having to endure struggle is the intrinsic nature of man in relation to life. We wonder whether it is possible to remain rooted, rise, and bloom by accepting life's trials while remaining our true authentic selves.

The Process of Accepting my Trial

I used to cry whenever I was left at the hospital as a child because it was not a place of familiarity. From the sterile bed to the bright lights, the environment at the hospital was different from home. I was surrounded by faces covered with masks instead of the warm smiles of my parents and brothers. I thought it made most sense to recover from illnesses within your own home—a place of familiarity, with your loved ones—than in a hospital. I did not understand why I had to be admitted to the hospital every year. I saw no point in the struggle, nor benefit to the isolation. I could not understand being left alone, hurt, broken, and confused. This feeling of brokenness slowly developed into frustration where I felt anger not only over my circumstance, but also towards the world and those around me.

I thought that my emotions, like the environment I was in, were not in my control. I wanted to get out and recover. I wanted to be in my own room and bed. I wanted to be around my brothers and wake up to my mother telling us to get ready for school. I longed to wait for my father to get back home from work and be the first one to greet him. I wanted to go *home* so much that a single minute at the hospital felt like hours, and the endless cries from the children in the other room only added to the agony.

'How can I heal from this place?'
'How can I recover and grow stronger, facing all this?'

The questions increased with time.

'How long do I have to be stuck here?'
'What is the point of all this?'
'Why did You leave me?'
'Why me?'

I cried to the extent that I could not cry anymore and was consumed with fury. I did not know how long I could mourn, realizing that my anger took a lot of energy from me. Eventually, I did not have the strength to feel upset anymore, so my emotions settled into numbness. I later refused to feel and watched each day pass, expecting never to be allowed home. I began to believe that I should realize that I had no choice but to stay and just accept the hospital as my place of residence.

This realization led me to find other ways to cope. I grew distant and almost detached from my surroundings. I often stared at the hospital's picture-painted walls and drifted away in creating my own reality. The blue-painted strokes on the walls were now tides of the sea that were ready to take me. My cold-steeled hospital bed was actually a boat that previously sailed many adventures. I was that little girl who began to imagine a different world and place— an environment where I was free.

My coping mechanism began to slowly wear off as my imagination ran dry from my never-changing environment. I escaped into storybooks for children placed within the hospital ward, where the story plots for each character felt like a new adventure. I found a new sense of freedom within the pages but would dread the end, knowing it meant that I had to put the book down and return to *my reality*.

Every time, it felt like I was popping that blissful bubble of mine. Eventually, I began to feel dissatisfied over some of what I read, due to the picture-perfect, happily-ever-after narrative. It did not feel real even though I wanted to escape from what was real. I realized that deluding myself as a coping mechanism was not effective in the long run, but at the same time, I could not deny how books were helping me. I became curious to read about real-life people. Characters that lived out their dreams but also experienced hardships. I wanted their reality to help me with my reality. I yearned to find comfort in witnessing how they underwent struggles but eventually overcame them, and how everything turned out okay for them in the end. I longed to trust that, in the same way, everything would turn out for the best with me, too.

Noticing my eagerness to read, and the number of questions that I would ask, my parents and elders gave me books on the stories of the Prophets. Books on historical figures instead of fictional characters increased my anticipation to delve into their lives simply because they were real. The stories of the Prophets were unlike others because I got to see how they—as individuals—went through the process of not only enduring pain but also tasting relief; the process of getting lost but being found; the state of having to face difficulty but later being rescued. These stories enabled me to see not only the hardships of the Prophets but also the hope within their difficulties. I was momentarily able to feel relief, until tears resurfaced again. The tears that I now shed were not out of despair but rather release. I began to let myself not only *feel* something again, but also be more open to accepting my situation, and not let anger engulf me. I was now attempting to not retreat in denial, but rather to observe the environment that I was in to better understand the plans of Allah ﷻ.

This change in perspective led me to be more absorbed whenever reading books on the Prophets. Whenever I would look up from my book, it felt like I had a fresh pair of eyes. The lessons within their lives provided insight. I shared these insights with my mom, and she would refer to their stories to help me see that whatever hardship we face is temporary. This life in itself is brief. This stopped me from dwelling on how I felt alone, or how the children were crying. I was redirected to see that I was not alone in my difficulties. I was shown how the most noble of humans in our past experienced hardships but later found relief. The awareness of how others experienced trials led me to notice the children around me who were in worse conditions than me. I realized that what I was going through was nothing compared to them.

There was a four-year-old boy who could not sit down and was in bed the whole time that I was there. I grew curious about him because I noticed that his parents rarely visited him. He had been there from the moment he was born. He had been there for four years when I had merely been there for four months. Whenever I felt like crying, I would get out of my isolated room to visit him, to look beyond what I was going through.

My mom once explained after we visited him that when it comes to worldly matters, we should look at those going through more difficult hardships than us, to increase our gratitude. When it comes to our character, we should look at those higher in piety, to inspire us to be better. This concept heightened my awareness of both the hardships of others and my reactions to my own difficulties. It taught me to respond to my trial better and focus on growth instead of complaining.

My mom telling me about children around the world, enduring different forms of hardships, made it easier to accept my trial. This acceptance led me to feel grateful for having my parents during the day.

My mom had to leave for home at 8 p.m. so that she could be there for my two younger brothers, who were five and three at the time. I wanted my brothers to have our mom, but I also wanted the whole family together. Being left behind was a test to see whether I genuinely accepted my trial.

The lights went out at 9 p.m., so I had an hour to myself. An hour to practise acceptance through gratitude. The nurse would enter my room at around 8:55 p.m. for my injection. I practised acceptance by readily holding out my arm instead of pulling away. I did so by thinking of children going through more than me.

'Prophet Yūsuf ﷺ as a child accepted separation from his family, so I should accept,' I thought.

'Prophet Yūsuf ﷺ expressed his feelings in supplication to Allah ﷻ, so I can express too.' I gazed towards the ceiling, waiting for that sting within my veins to fade.

One day my mother introduced to me the concept of thanking Allah ﷻ by saying 'Alḥamdulillāh' not only in good times but also in bad times. I could not understand why Muslims thank Allah ﷻ in bad times, but I was curious to understand. I had become open to taking life in instead of shutting it out. I was eager to let my circumstances build me up instead of breaking me down.

I was ready to accept and grow.

I felt guilty for previously being ungrateful and letting my emotions loose. I did not know why I had not accepted it sooner. Ingratitude is, however, necessary to discover gratitude. The process of being admitted to the hospital aided my growth by allowing me to learn life's reality: that hardships are temporary and are there to equip us to gain insights. This is why Muslims say 'Alḥamdulillāh' during difficult times because difficulties help us develop perspective. This does not mean that we do not allow ourselves the time to attempt escaping a test. It is a natural human instinct. The emotions of grief, anger, loss, and denial are all part of the human experience—a process we must go through to find strength.

Acceptance of life's reality does not mean that we do not embrace our own innate reality. We *feel* when enduring hardships. This is not weakness, rather it is vulnerability.

Vulnerability may appear as a weakness.

The reason for this is because vulnerability is our raw feelings that are not in our control. Vulnerability, therefore, is our inability to keep whatever is happening within our hearts and minds under wrap. It is regarded as our failure to toughen up.

Those vulnerable are, therefore, considered weak.

According to Merriam Webster's Dictionary, vulnerability comes from the Latin root word *vulnerare*. The meaning is 'to wound' as in being 'capable of being wounded'. We are, therefore, 'open to attack or damage' due to being unguarded and being readily available to approach. On the other hand, weakness is defined as 'the inability to withstand attack or wounding'. These definitions demonstrate that being vulnerable cannot be a weakness. It can only be a strength, due to the ability to be open and withstand hurt.

In scenarios that cause pain and grief, it is natural to feel hurt and have the urge to complain. We may break down. Breaking down does not mean that we can never build ourselves up, just as feeling weak does not mean we can never find strength. It is in a place of weakness that we first find strength. Strength can be found in *what* we complain about and *whom* we complain to about our suffering.

Prophet Ya'qūb ﷺ faced grief after being separated from his son Yūsuf ﷺ. He embraced his innate nature as a human while accepting life's reality—illustrating how we ought to react toward a trial.

After being separated from his son, Ya'qūb ﷺ said,

> *'I only complain of my grief and sorrow to Allah.'*
>
> (*Yūsuf* 12: 86)

The Prophets found life hard. They complained, but to Allah ﷻ. They acknowledged what they were feeling to their loved ones, but they did not lament. They recognized their needs and nature as humans.

The complaints of Yaʿqūb ﷺ were not out of ingratitude, instead were an expression of release and reliance. He was aware of how trials were there to raise us up. How it was an opportunity for growth and not defeat. The complaints from Prophets were never over their circumstances but rather their feelings—the pain and struggle that emerged due to their circumstances. They did not deny nor numb their intrinsic nature. They knew that the endurance of this pain was a means to discover strength.

It is instinctive to feel at a loss whenever we lose something, and habitual to want to return to familiarity. Ibn Asakir reported that Ādam ﷺ grieved for sixty years for his loss of Paradise, a place where he hoped to return. He then spent seventy years seeking forgiveness for his mistakes. He spent the remainder of his life focused on his role as vicegerent on Earth.[1]

The first stage shows the grief Ādam ﷺ had when taken away from familiarity to a place of unfamiliarity. He was taken away from a place of ease to one of hardship. Ādam ﷺ gave himself time to mourn his loss. Grief, or the feeling of loss, is not wrong. It is not an act of weakness but shows how we are innately weak and are bound to feel despair. We must go through the necessary process of grief to heal, and later find that strength to grow. This process may take time and we might make mistakes along the way, but the second stage of the life of Ādam ﷺ shows that we

---

1   (Ibn Kathir 2014, 20)

can seek forgiveness for our actions and reactions; it shows hope. His third stage demonstrates the possibility to move beyond grief and rise to our roles on this Earth.

It is possible to heal and grow *during* our hardships. Ādam ﷺ was still on this Earth; he was still enduring his trial. He was placed on this Earth—in this trial—to grow.

The descent of Ādam ﷺ to Earth was not out of degradation; instead, it was an <u>honorary descent</u> for him to learn and grow.

Trials are not there to degrade us; they exist to honour us towards growth.

Allah ﷻ created Ādam ﷺ not just to worship Him, but for him to learn and grow.

> '*Allah **taught** Ādam all the names of everything.*'
> (*al-Baqarah* 2: 31)

We, as the descendants of Ādam ﷺ, are put in this world to learn and grow.

Our circumstances may not change. This does not mean we cannot fulfill our purpose while going through difficulty. Like Ādam ﷺ, we can find that internal strength to fulfill our purpose during our trials. It is possible to bloom.

We may not see that the purpose of our trial is growth, nor notice the process, but the example of Yūsuf ﷺ can help us appreciate the wisdom of recognizing the process at the right time. As a young boy, Yūsuf ﷺ saw a dream wherein he was promised to be raised in ranks. It foretold that he would one day be a leader over his parents and brothers. Shortly after having this dream, he was sold as a slave.

We might question, at this point in the story, how Yūsuf 🕊 as a slave would end up a leader. Our focus would be the immeasurable pain, betrayal, and loneliness Yūsuf 🕊 felt. The unattainability of him being a leader after being sold as a slave. The prophecy of his dream, however, could not have become a reality if he had not been separated from his father as a boy. He had to be bought as a slave by one of the king's ministers in Egypt to be raised in that household with influential figures. This environment prepared him for his growth before reuniting him with his family. This was where he was meant to be planted to grow.

Allah 🕊 says,

And the one from Egypt who bought him said to his wife, 'Make his residence comfortable. Perhaps he will benefit us, or we will adopt him as a son.' And thus, We **established Yūsuf in the land** *that We* **might teach him the interpretations** *of events. And* **Allah is predominant over His affair**, *but most of the people do not know.*

(*Yūsuf* 12: 21)

Our trial may be painful and challenging but accepting both the hardship and our nature as humans facilitates the process of growth.

The hardships the Prophets faced were necessary for them to endure, grow, and rise. They are examples for us to know how to unleash our strength from within.

Being admitted to the hospital and going through all those emotions was a necessary process for me. It gave me time to discover the difficulties of the Prophets, the world, and our nature as humans. This equipped me to endure the challenges in life and compile this book—a means to share how I discovered strength while living with disabilities. There are many times when I feel weak. Still, my physical state is a constant reminder that we are vulnerable and are meant to find strength from our vulnerabilities.

We are destined to rise from our hardships.

We are meant to find that strength from within us and bloom.

Chapter 3

Entrapment Due to Anxieties

Hardships are there for us to grow, but we fear the unknown. We are afraid of what out-of-control adversity might happen next. We accept that we face moments of weakness through complaints and wanting to flee a test. We know this is out of being unsure of how long we can endure our tests. We may ultimately survive but face anguish over the thought of possibly having to experience an even more severe difficulty. There is an internal battle of whether we should continue to try our best in living, or retreat and hide.

Many times, we choose to hide. We hide out of overwhelming fear and anxiety.

Anxiety occurs after an enduring loss—and the fear of experiencing that pain again—or when we try something new.

These realms of unfamiliarity may foster anxieties that could grow if not dealt with or talked about. They grow to such an extent that agitation could cause panic, so that instead of living, one is paralyzed with fear.

My Entrapment due to Anxieties

I did not have to be repeatedly admitted to the hospital for pneumonia after I started using the breathing machine from the age of eight. I did, however, gradually lose physical strength. By the age of ten, it was harder to climb stairs on my own compared to before. I had always struggled climbing stairs, but by my teens, I needed increased support, until eventually, the only way up the stairs was having someone carry me. The loss of physical strength gradually progressed to the extent that I needed help getting up from the chair. In my early twenties, I started finding it harder to walk. I became consumed with anxiety, fearing I was losing all physical strength, that suddenly I needed support even when walking. I could not tell if it was physically harder to walk, or if it was anxiety, triggering fear. It appeared like I was going through a drastic physical change, but this new reality caused a more radical shift internally. I became fixated on trying to maintain strength and was confused over my increased struggles. *Why was my strength not under control?* This led me to not want to face or try new things, even though my physical state could allow it.

I was able to walk, but I convinced myself that it was harder than it really was. I was able to breathe, but I felt so constricted that I wanted to lie down with my breathing machine.

My world—my reality—felt altered.

I did not know how to continue living to the fullest, especially since I had to face physical struggles from the moment that I got out of bed. Everything agitated me, from taking my first step to being around people.

What heightened my anxiety was the fact that my physical disability[1] was at first undetectable since the weakness of my muscles was not evident by my appearance. I was able to disguise myself by standing within a crowd, but the moment I was asked to keep pace with someone, I did not know how to disclose that I could not keep up. I was unsure how to not alarm others by letting them know that a slight shove could make me fall and that once on the ground, I needed help getting up.

As a child, there were many times when I had to explain to my peers on the playground that I could not keep up with them. Most of the time, however, they would think that I was making up excuses. There were some who were hurt that I did not want to play. They would walk away crushed, and by the time I could reply, they were too far away for me to reach them.

I felt responsible for letting them down—a responsibility that increased my anxiety.

I appeared 'normal' but there was a war within me. A conflict that left me picking up life's pieces to make sense of everything—from the world to my body, and most importantly, my mind.

---

1 A person is considered 'disabled' due to dependency, but we are all in essence dependent on Allah ﷻ with different ranges of abilities and dependencies. There is no clear-cut categorization, which gives a sense of ambiguity as to what determines one to be 'disabled'. Stigma towards disability, however, exists and can be an everyday reality that people with disabilities and their carers face.

These are the steps I took to cope with my anxieties:

1. REMEMBER LIFE'S REALITY

I tried to understand the sudden change in my life and why I was scared. I found assurance in this verse:

'And We will surely test you with something of fear and hunger and a loss of wealth and lives and fruits, but give good tidings to the patient.'
(*al-Baqarah* 2: 155)

Allah ﷻ will surely test us with fear. It is both expected and normal to feel scared. There is nothing wrong with being anxious over losing our loved ones or enduring something difficult. We are encouraged to be patient through acceptance.

I did not know what patience meant, though. It was annoying whenever anyone told me to be patient, especially when I was already trying. I knew patience meant recognizing unforeseen good in our tests, but that did not negate the uneasiness that I felt, nor the struggles I endured. Tolerance does not take that anxiety and feeling of entrapment away.

2. ENGAGE THE 5 SENSES

Anxiety is an internal battle.

I get triggered by anxiety when I cannot breathe so, to overcome this anxiety, I keep essential oils within easy reach. Engaging my sense of smell reminds me that I can breathe. This releases me from my anxiety and allows me to carry on with my everyday tasks without feeling the need to escape.

There are times when I do not only engage my sense of smell but simultaneously look at something within my environment to find comfort. I started doing this after noticing the mention of 'coolness of the eye'—قُرَّةَ أَعْيُنٍ—within the Qur'an, ranging from loved ones to objects. This concept indicates the possibility of finding comfort just by a mere glance.

'Coolness of the eyes' from objects referenced within the Qur'an would be the stream and dates for Maryam ☙ during childbirth. Maryam ☙ was anxious not only because of going through delivery alone but also because of feeling entrapped for having to explain her situation to people within her community.

Maryam ☙ said,

*'Oh, **I wish I had died** before this and was in **oblivion**, **forgotten**.'*
(Maryam 19: 23)

Entrapment from anxiety causes us to want to disappear from existence altogether.

Allah ☙—through Jibrīl ☙—redirects the focus of Maryam ☙ to release her from anxiety.

*'Do not grieve; your Lord has provided **beneath** you a stream. And **shake** toward you the trunk of the palm tree; it will drop upon you ripe, fresh dates. So **eat and drink and be contented [cool your eyes]**.'*
(Maryam 19: 24–26)

The redirection of her sight shifted her focus from how she felt. This trained her mind to endure her pain by engaging her sight. She was further released from anxiety by busying herself with a task: the task of shaking the tree, despite the difficulty of childbirth. *The sense of touch.* The act of putting our minds on a task momentarily makes us forget the source of our anxiety. Maryam 🌸 then ate and drank, thus engaging her sense of taste. Food and drink were 'coolness' to her because they aided with her childbirth—the source of her anxiety.

However, there will also be times when engaging our senses feels like too much effort. It may be that physical exhaustion triggers anxiety. This is an indication to rest our senses by napping. This can replenish both our physical and internal strength to help us better tackle anxiety.

3. RECOGNIZE THE TRIGGERS

Our anxiety is triggered by whispers of self-doubt. This could lead to our downfall. So it helps to know what triggers our doubts. I realized that I would be triggered with doubts whenever I tried to grow or start something new. I did not believe these thoughts, but I kept having them against my will.

It helped me to recognize that we also have someone who does not want us to rise but instead wants us to self-sabotage—Satan.

Allah 🕌 says,

> 'Indeed, Satan is an **enemy to you**, so take him as an enemy.'
>
> (*Fāṭir* 35: 6)

In a scenario where I felt my thoughts were against my will, it helped me to know what Allah ﷻ wants us to think and what Satan wants us to believe. Distinguish what is wanted from both. It is Satan's mission to hinder us from believing in Allah ﷻ and the potential He has given us. Giving in to Satan's mission will lead us to stay still and not move forward. It is natural to have fear when enduring difficulty. Still, severe worries, due to repetitive doubt, can lead to sabotaging our potential—the potential that Allah ﷻ wants us to fulfill.

Anxieties may also occur due to chemical imbalances within our brains[2] caused by traumas experienced in the past. We may need time and professional help to recover. Some of my anxieties are biologically related due to my heart being underdeveloped and naturally beating faster. It helped me to distinguish the two because non-medical prolonged hand-gripping anxiety can be triggered by Satan. This is a tactic he uses to stop us from seeing clearly and reaching our potential.

Understanding this reality made it easier to control the battle within my mind.

Prophet Ayyūb ﷺ endured health challenges and the loss of his loved ones and wealth. He felt so defeated at one point that he invoked Allah ﷻ, saying:

---

2   Some anxieties are medically related, where it is encouraged to seek help and treatment, and have a support system. It is not out of weakness of faith but rather a biological aspect that needs proper care. It may be due to a chemical imbalance or an involuntarily fast-paced heartbeat. Those battling with anxiety may indeed have strong faith and be more than capable of finding their strength from within.

*'Verily! **Satan has touched me with distress** [by losing my health]
and **torment** [by losing my wealth]!'*

(*Ṣād* 38: 41)

Ayyūb 🕮 did not complain about losing health or wealth. He
complained about how Satan had afflicted him with distress by
exploiting him through whispers over how severe his condition was.
Ayyūb 🕮 had natural distress. Satan, however, manipulates our
natural distress, pushing us towards ingratitude and impatience.
Ayyūb 🕮 recognized this tactic and requested help from Allah 🕮
to ease his distress.

The distress of Ayyūb 🕮 shows how it is normal to feel torment,
anguish, and anxiety whenever enduring a trial. It is encouraged
to seek help not by complaining about external events that are
happening to us, but rather by expressing *how we feel internally.*
Simply asking Allah 🕮 to help overcome the distress provides a
release that will bring us comfort.

That release can help us cope with anxiety and put things into
perspective.

It helped me.

A few months after my marriage, and before our *walīmah*
(wedding feast) ceremony, I expressed to my husband how I felt
anxious because being a bride meant that I had to talk to some who
have always looked down on me.

*'I read articles that brides usually feel anxious, but I am a bride in a
wheelchair, so I am seventy times more anxious,'* I exclaimed.

My husband looked over, waiting for me to finish.

'Why anxious when Allah ﷻ is with you—this isn't you but Satan meddling with you.'

What he said stuck.

My triggers of self-doubt were not what I actually thought. I considered it an honour to get married and did not look at my disability as a barrier, but as an asset. It would not matter if others looked down because I already felt honoured. *My husband knew this of me.* Allah ﷻ has allowed marriage for those with disabilities. Prophet Muhammad ﷺ actively tried to find spouses for Companions with disabilities, like Julaybib ؓ. Companions with disabilities were honoured within authentic Islamic history.

This recognition of Satan triggering my self-doubt over my actual thoughts—and acknowledging what Allah ﷻ wants for me—helped me break free.

4. CONFIDE IN LOVED ONES

When I confided to my family about my anxiety regarding walking, I discovered that I was *not* getting physically weaker, as I had thought. I was drinking a new tea that was higher in caffeine when I first got triggered. I also had dizzy spells and, due to the high doses of caffeine, I was not getting enough sleep. I even spent more time than usual writing, sometimes four to six hours straight. This affected my blood circulation, which affected my walking. My heart naturally beats faster than average and drinking that high-caffeinated tea only increased my heartbeat. I could not figure out what was happening on my own. It helped to have my family analyze the causes of triggers and eliminate them.

I simultaneously started physiotherapy sessions at home. We discovered that I was using the wrong muscles when it came to walking. I was neither walking nor standing the right way, so I needed to train myself using different sets of muscles. This triggered my anxiety again because it meant using a different—and unfamiliar—set of exercises. Still, figuring out my triggers with the help of my family, by listing the changing factors in my life, put things in perspective for me. Anyone would feel anxious and find it harder to walk if they continuously used the muscles that I was using. The muscles people typically use to walk were my weakest muscles, but I began training them. I have not returned to walking on my own, but the triggers have decreased.

There is no shame in confiding our anxieties and accepting help to figure out how to cope. We are encouraged to seek help because when we do so, we see that things are not so bad.

Breaking Free from Anxiety

I got to discover that it is possible to live productively while having anxiety. But could I fully break free from it?

My anxiety grew from trying to control both my physical strength as well as the anxiety that emerged from doing so. It helped me turn to Allah ﷻ because when I raised my hands to Him, the struggle to keep my hands raised up showed me that I was trying to control something that was only in the control of Allah ﷻ. Hardships were never meant for us to control.

Allah ﷻ says,

> *'And **Allah wants to lighten your burdens**, for **mankind** was created weak.'*
>
> (*al-Nisā'* 4: 28)

Allah ﷻ tells us that He wants to lighten our burdens **before** showing us the reality that mankind was created weak. We are vulnerable and find things heavy. We are only meant to control what is within our ability—our inner selves.

Life's trials may crack us open, but fixating on the crack, and remaining in anxiety over potential future cracks, only prevents us from coming out of our seeds towards growth. Internal cultivation allows us to live a life built on purpose; it leads us to a life where we strive to bloom.

The Qur'an relates explicitly that whoever recites the prayer that Yūnus ﷺ made when he was in the whale—which encourages us to shift our focus to what is in our control—would have their anxieties removed from Allah ﷻ and their prayers answered.

Allah ﷻ says,

> *'We **answered his call** and **delivered him from the distress** [from the **belly of the fish** and **from the darkness**]. And thus, **We do deliver (save) the believers.'***
>
> (*al-Anbiyā'* 21: 88)

Allah ﷻ promises that He will deliver us to safety whenever we find ourselves alone and in darkness, due to life's trials. We must believe in Him, turn to Him, and build a life of purpose by trying our best to improve in things over which we have control.

The remembrance of the beautiful Names of Allah[3] ﷻ in supplications helped me break free from my anxiety. Each Name serves a purpose in helping us understand how He can do all things.

Allah ﷻ can hear our worries as al-Samī' (the Hearer of all) and can answer as al-Mujīb (the Responder of prayers). He can guide us as al-Hādī (the Guide) whenever we are confused, and He can bring us out from the darkness as al-Nūr (the Light). He can break us free from distress as al-Bāsiṭ (the Reliever) whenever we feel overwhelmed. He can grant us peace as al-Salām (the Source of peace) whenever we are not at ease.

He is able—and the only One able—to do all things. So when anxious, remember Him.

He can ultimately help us break free.

The key to breaking free from the entrapment of anxieties is to have our hearts rest with ease.

After all, Allah ﷻ promises those who believe:

'Verily in the remembrance of Allah do hearts find rest.'
(*al-Ra'd* 13: 28)

This is our key.

---

3 'Hearts that Remember' is a book I later wrote under Iman Publications on Allah (SWT)'s names. It originally was a compilation of poems on all of Allah (SWT)'s 99 names.

Chapter 4

From Fear to Courage

Allah is near.

He is there for us to call upon using His Beautiful Names. He rescues us from distress and releases us from our trials. He is there, but fear remains with us. We try to rise, even though we tumble. We push forward when our hearts rumble. But all that is felt is fear and the pacing of the heart that thuds louder with every beat.

How can we move forward with courage?

Is it possible to do so when we are pulled back by fear?

Allah says,

*'Indeed, I am **near**. I **respond to the invocation** of the supplicant when He calls upon Me. So let them **respond to Me [by obedience]** and **believe in Me** that they may be **rightly guided**.'*
(*al-Baqarah* 2: 186)

The way to hear the call to courage loudly and clearly is to focus on understanding the call of the Prophets. Their call is the message of Allah ﷻ.

We can live with fear—as the Prophets have shown us—but we are encouraged to *tame* our fears so that we can use them as our drive to respond to the One behind the call, Allah ﷻ.

Respond to the call of courage with trust that Allah ﷻ will guide us in the best way out of our difficulties.

He will not just take us out but *guide* us out.

We will be guided out only if we take the steps towards obedience by answering the call, the message brought by the Prophets.

Ready to Answer the Call to Courage?

There are many days when lying down with my breathing machine makes me feel like I am buried beneath the ground. There are days when I do not have it together because of my physical weakness. It is on such days I can find strength by just appreciating that life is cracking me open. I appreciate that I am alive and can breathe.

The following prayer gives me the strength to stand, face my fears, and answer my call to courage:

'There is no power and no strength except with Allah.'

(لَا حَوْلَ وَلَا قُوَّةَ إِلَّا بِاَللهِ)

This prayer acknowledges that I am weak both physically and emotionally. It reminds me that I cannot face anything without the help of Allah ﷻ for He, as al-Qawwiy, is the Giver of strength. He has power and strength over my fears. The external things that I fear are nothing compared to Allah ﷻ. They have no control over me if I believe that Allah ﷻ will help.

At times we may feel that despite our belief in Allah ﷻ and doing good through obedience, fear still has a tight grip on us. We may feel that our strength is draining. Strength, like courage, comes in waves. We are momentarily pulled back only to return with more force.

It is hard to leave our comfort zone, but when we do, we realize that we have not truly lived. Life is waiting to be unleashed. We do not experience the world to the fullest when on the sidelines. We are planted in this world to do good. We will not know the potential within us—His gifts to us—if we live in fear. There are miracles inside us that are waiting to happen.

Do not be held back by negative experiences that result in fear. *Be a positive experience for others instead.*

Do not feel shaken over negative experiences. *Rise from them instead.*

Allah ﷻ promised that believers would be shaken. So who could say being shaken is a bad thing?

Breathe.

Step into the light. Seize this realization. The Mercy of Allah ﷻ is always there, especially during difficulties. He is waiting for us to answer the call to courage. There is no one more pleased whenever we attempt to grow. He is The Most Sincere and will not abandon us when in difficulty.

"The question is, will we abandon ourselves?"

Or will we answer the call to courage?

Allah ﷻ does not abandon those who answer His call to courage. He, as al-Walī, is our Protecting Friend.

He did not let Mūsā ﷺ down when facing Pharaoh. Similarly, He will not let us down.

Find strength from Him to answer **His call** *to courage.*

He will grant us strength from within.

I promise.

My battle from fear to courage

The story of Mūsā ﷺ helps me in answering the call to courage when facing my everyday fears.

Prophet Mūsā ﷺ exemplifies courage in times of fear?

He had different layers of fear when instructed to return to Egypt and free his people:

- Internal fear of facing harm from Pharaoh.
- External fear of his unclear speech due to his physical disability.

Mūsā ﷺ says,

> 'My Lord! I have accidentally killed a man among them, and **I fear that they will kill me**. And my brother Hārūn is more eloquent in speech than me, so send him with me as a helper to confirm me. Verily, **I fear that they will deny me**.'
>
> (al-Qaṣaṣ 28: 33–34)

Then Mūsā ﷺ marched forth, despite his fears, solely because he wanted to obey Allah ﷻ.

Allah ﷻ has revealed the fears of Mūsā ﷺ to show us that we also can tackle both internal and external fears.

Below are steps that show how Mūsā ﷺ responded to fear by answering the call to courage:

1. Admit Fears to Allah ﷻ and Request Ease

Mūsā ﷺ said,

> 'O my Lord! **Expand me my breast** and **ease my task** for me.'
>
> (ṬāHā 20: 25–26)

Mūsā ﷺ admitted his fears. The chest area is constricted whenever one is stressed, overwhelmed, or scared. Mūsā's admitting his fears and requesting that Allah ﷻ expand his chest, is an act of trust, reliance, and belief. Fear is not a weakness of faith. It strengthens faith based on *how* one responds. Mūsā ﷺ took a step towards courage when he was open about his fears. It was his process of attaining strength from within to stand strong in the face of difficulty.

2. Demonstrate the Willingness to Obey

Mūsā ﷺ demonstrated the willingness to obey Allah ﷻ by requesting ease for his task. The fear of not obeying Allah was far greater than facing Pharaoh.

We must acknowledge our fears to Allah ﷻ with the intention of obeying him. Request help to answer the call.

Let the fear of not answering the call of Allah ﷻ be greater than the fear of anything else.

This is how we continue to stand.

Allah ﷻ grants ease when obeying Him even if we are stricken with fear. He does so by giving us internal strength. This is demonstrated through the mother of Mūsā when she found out that her baby— Mūsā ﷺ —had reached Pharaoh's palace, despite her obeying Allah ﷻ.

Allah ﷻ explains,

> *'But there came to **be a void in the heart of the mother of Mūsā**: she was going **almost to disclose** his [case] <u>**had We not strengthened her heart [with faith]**</u> so that she might **remain a [firm] believer.'***

> (*al-Qaṣaṣ* 28: 10)

The mother of Mūsā ﷺ obeyed Allah ﷻ with trust but was tested with more fear. Allah ﷻ, however, strengthened her to remain firm as a believer. This additional strength was granted because she had previously obeyed. It was through obedience to Allah ﷻ—and being gifted with increased strength to aid her in continuously standing strong—that she pushed through her fear.

3. Seek Aid from Loved Ones

The story of Mūsā ﷺ gave me the strength to walk with aid. It helped me face the reality of acknowledging our limitations when facing fears and answering our call to courage.

Mūsā ﷺ said,

> 'And send my brother Hārūn — he is more eloquent in speech than I — so send him with me as **a helper to confirm [and strengthen me] for I fear** they may accuse me of falsehood.'
> (al-Qaṣaṣ 28: 34)

Mūsā ﷺ recognized his physical limitations and asked Allah ﷻ for help. Ask Allah ﷻ not only for *internal* help but also *for external* physical help. It is not an act of disobedience or weakness; it is a step toward answering the call. We naturally fear ineffectiveness due to our limitations. Still, it is courageous to reach out for help because it requires internal strength to be vulnerable. Recognition of needing aid does not mean avoiding responsibility. Mūsā ﷺ upheld the primary responsibility to deliver the message; he only requested the presence of Hārūn ﷺ to strengthen him when delivering the message. He trusted that Allah ﷻ would make his speech effective with aid.

Hārūn 🕮 must have known the fears of Mūsā 🕮. There is nothing wrong with sharing our worries with our loved ones. Acceptance of external help is not defeat—it is the acceptance of mercy from Allah 🕮.

For me, accepting assistance when walking—due to the fear that I may not be strong enough to do so on my own—was not a step back. It was a means to move forward.

4. TRUST IN A POSITIVE RESULT

Mūsā 🕮 trusted that Allah 🕮 would provide a good end for his answering the call to courage.

This is shown in his prayer when he requests a good end result:

*'My Lord, expand for me my breast **[with assurance]** and ease for me my task. And untie the knot from my tongue. That **they may understand my speech.'***

(*al-Anbiyā'* 20: 25-28)

Pray for the end result and trust that Allah 🕮 will allow what is best. The end goal for Mūsā 🕮 was for Pharaoh and his people to understand his speech. This hope gave him the confidence and courage to march forth.

5. PUSH THROUGH FEAR BY SHIFTING FOCUS ON BEING THERE FOR OTHERS

Mūsā 🕮 faced Pharaoh to free his people who were being oppressed. This was his drive. The main way I pushed through my fear with action is by being there for those in similar circumstances as me. Allah 🙌 compensates us for taking steps towards our call to courage despite our fear; He provides us with something that strengthens us. Allah 🙌 does this to aid us in answering our call out of obedience and being there for others. Mūsā 🙌 had fear because he struggled with speech. Allah 🙌, in turn, strengthened him with a gift that no other Prophet was blessed with before him: the ability to directly converse with Him.

I have a fear of walking, but writing to encourage others going through hardships helps me unearth that strength from within to carry on. It is a gift from Allah 🙌.

He has prepared a gift for every single one of us.

6. REPEL FEAR BY DOING GOOD

When Mūsā 🙌 first left Egypt out of fear and was stranded without food or shelter, he came across the daughters of Prophet Shuʿayb 🙌. They were struggling to carry water from the well. Mūsā 🙌 helped them despite being in need himself and returned to the shade under a tree afterwards. There he made a prayer to Allah 🙌.

Allah 🙌 reveals,

> ʻSo he watered [their flocks] for them; then he went back to the shade and said, "My Lord, indeed I am, for whatever **good You would send down to me, in need."** Then one of the two women came to him walking with shyness. She said, "Indeed, my father invites you that **he may reward you** for having watered for us." So when he came to him and related to him the story, he said, "**Fear not.** You have escaped from the wrongdoing people."'

(al-Qaṣaṣ 28: 24–5)

Strive to do good when scared. The act of reaching out to help others pulls us out from fear to places we never imagined.

When I was invited to give a talk in Singapore back in 2014, I was in my early twenties and a new writer. I was scared because not only was I requested to travel but also to speak abroad. It requires extensive planning for those with physical disabilities to plan a day-trip within their hometown; going overseas can be unfathomable. There is the fear that circumstances might change midway and require one to navigate health issues within an unfamiliar environment. My parents rented an extra breathing machine just in case my home-used breathing machine broke down. They made sure that I completely rested in bed for a few days before we travelled.

Travelling to speak brought with it another layer of fear: the befuddlement of not knowing whether I would get sick on the day or find difficulty sleeping the night before. At that point, I had never given a talk outside of an educational environment for more than fifteen minutes. I was not sure what was manageable. I expressed my fears to those who invited me. They said that they were aware of my disability and wanted me to talk about my life with disabilities. They wanted me to openly share and be the person that I was in my writing.

At first, I did not want to go, but the thought of obeying Allah ﷻ with trust and reaching out to people for His sake made it easier to face the situation. I feared that my speech would not be clear, but I remembered Mūsā ﷺ trying with his disability. Everything is in the hands of Allah ﷻ. He is the One that moves hearts. He will help in times of fear, especially if we are striving to help others for His sake.

Allah ﷻ did help.

I prepared a short video on top of the twenty-five-minute live speech presentation. My Uncle Jalal—as a toastmaster—polished my script; my brothers filmed shots for me to add subtitles in; I used PowerPoint as my aid for the live session; and my parents helped me walk on stage. Allah's help came in many ways.

I spoke standing up because I was not sure if I could inhale as deeply when speaking in a low wheelchair. I did not know the way I felt most comfortable. I went through the external fear of whether I could balance standing for long and effectively speaking. I worried about losing my balance midway and being unable to complete the task with ease.

I was also scared of what I had to talk about: my life with physical disabilities. I had never had to *talk* about my life with disabilities openly before. I was only beginning to write about it, so openly speaking about it required getting out of my shell. I did not know if I could publicly share the internal battles I had faced while at the hospital. I did not know if I could own my experiences—my vulnerabilities—on stage.

There was both the external fear from physical hardship and the internal fear of whether my talk would resonate with those who did not have disabilities. I worried that I would be uncovering my story—my pain—with the response being pity instead of the audience hearing the message of strength and trust towards Allah ﷻ.

I was scared, but Allah ﷻ was there.

My parents helped me stand behind the podium, and I rehearsed the prayer Mūsā ﷺ had made for clarity and ease in speech. Silence filled the room. Fear gripped me tighter as I scanned those before me. I unclenched my jaw, and the words soon flowed. There were smiles and nods, and some tears with them. I cracked a joke and forgot about the fears that had previously gripped me.

I answered the call—completed my task—from my heart's core.

After I finished my speech, my father carried me off the stage. My mother gripped my hand with a smile. My parents helped me walk back, but before reaching our seats in the front row, there was a tide. The audience was up, ready to greet me. Strangers that were my sisters in faith warmly hugged me. I let go of my father's hand, and my mother carved her free arm behind me for balance and support as I hugged my sisters with my free arm. I was afraid of the fall, but I had a sea of sisters greeting me from their cores.

There was one sister who brought her grandmother and translated what I said to her into Malay. She said her grandmother was on her way to greet me but had been pulled back into the tide. I glanced to see her grandmother at a distance attempting to walk. She was like me—had two sisters as her aid.

Watching her pulled me into walking forward.

'This is why I came,' I thought.

The faster the grandmother walked, the quicker I paced with my mother's support. I let go of my mother's hand and extended both of my arms, ready to hug the grandmother. I took a step forward, terrified that I might fall, but it did not matter. I wrapped my arms around the grandmother as I felt my mother's hand supporting me to stand. The grandmother hugged me more. I leaned my head on her shoulder and hugged her while looking at my mother with a smile. I was overwhelmed, humbled, and in awe. How beautifully Allah ﷻ helps and replies. I was moved by how the grandmother walked to greet me despite her difficulty. How she came to attend, despite not understanding English.

Her heart understood what I wanted to say.

Allah ﷻ truly helps.

The story of Mūsā ﷺ gave me the strength to physically try despite my fears.

His story not only guides us on how to cope with physical difficulties but how to have hope when we are scared. Hope allows us to answer the call to courage. Turn to Allah ﷻ with fear *and* hope. The root word for *courage* is *cor*—which is the Latin word for heart. Thus, courage means 'to speak one's mind by telling one's heart'. Mūsā ﷺ poured what was on his mind by telling Allah ﷻ all that was in his heart. Whatever he felt, including his fears and owning his vulnerabilities, he shared with Allah ﷻ. This is how Mūsā ﷺ moved from fear to courage.

This is how we all can answer the call of courage.

Chapter 5

From Guilt to Forgiveness of the Self

I was only fifteen years old when I lay on the operating table before my surgery for multiple scoliosis.

The doctor held my hand to find my veins and insert the needle. He attempted this several times, but my veins were hard to find. When he went to the other corner of the room to find some essential equipment, I was left alone to think about how I had been for the previous few months. I had chosen to be guarded with family members by refusing to face or talk about my feelings, due to the doctors telling us that there was only a 20% survival rate for this operation. My lungs and heart were weak so it was hard to know whether my body could withstand this surgery. But more harm was expected if I did *not* undergo this surgery due to the severity of my spinal curve and the added pressure on my lungs and heart. I had no way out and decided that it was better to take the risk of undergoing surgery.

During those few months before the surgery, I coped by carrying on with my life and pretending as if everything was okay. I went to school and came home only to go to my room. I did not know how to react, so I hid behind my walls. My body was present, but I was not fully there. I would smile but not wholeheartedly engage.

I thought this was strength.

Life behind my walls consisted of spending time on the computer. I realized that I did not fully experience a childhood that consisted of mindless playing, due to either not being able to catch up, being sick, or being hospitalized. Computer games eliminated the fear of not being able to catch up. They were a way to take my mind off things and have a tinge of normalcy. I told myself that the games were somewhat productive because they encouraged participants to earn, hunt for food, and cook. It required planning and thinking. My younger brothers wanted to come into my room and play, but that would just snap me back to reality. I did not want to be brought back to reality. This would mean acknowledging that I would soon have to leave them—like I often did when I was hospitalized in our childhood—but this time I knew there was a possibility that I would not return. I wanted to play with them, but I feared them getting more attached. My operation brought us back to our childhood of uncertainty. As their elder sister, I wanted to protect them from pain and safeguard them from feeling that their sister might be snatched away.

Whenever we were together in our early childhood, we masked our fears. Every cough or sneeze caused my brother—who is three years younger than me—to flinch. He rushed to get water and cover me with his jacket. The eight-year-old me reassured him that I was okay and not to tell our parents. We did not want to worry them, but at the same time, we both feared that my cough would turn into something more and that I would soon have to leave home.

Too often, however, we could not hide from our parents for long and my coughs would turn into pneumonia. My parents preparing to take me away became something expected. It was our yearly routine. I reassured my younger brothers—who were five and three at the time—but my father picking me up was him taking their sister away.

I whispered to my father as he carried me that I was okay and that there was no need for the hospital. I looked over his shoulder to glance at my brothers with a smile. I continued explaining to my father that I could recover at home. He kissed me but continued walking, and my brothers followed, tugging at him, asking why I had to be taken away. My mother held their hands and reassured us. The youngest started to cry. This led my other brother to sniffle back tears, followed by me frantically holding it together with smiles, so they would stay strong.

'I'll come home soon.' I smiled while knowing that once they were out of sight, tears would stream down my cheeks.

I wanted to play computer games with them when I was fifteen, but I knew that while we played, the three of us would have my operation on our minds. Our parents did talk to us, but our pain and fears were still there. Our parents did the best any parent could.

Still, playing games together just made it easier for reality to grip us to the ground. I had previously tried reassuring my brothers once they first got to know of the surgery, but I feared giving them false hope and empty promises that I would return from the operation in better health. I trusted that Allah ﷻ would help and not abandon us, but I did not know *what* was best in the plans of Allah ﷻ. *Did He want me alive to write this book?* I was scared of talking about Allah ﷻ and His decree to my brothers. Because if leaving this world was better for me at that age, I did not want my brothers to feel like Allah ﷻ took their sister away.

I never wanted them to feel resentful towards Allah ﷻ. Because of that, I preferred that they not be too attached before I left for the operation.

I thought that I was protecting them.

It was my way of coping.

My way of staying strong.

This was what I thought I needed to find strength and have them be strong.

...I was wrong.

I did not know that pushing my family away—especially my brothers—would later engulf me with guilt.

As I lay in the operating room, I could not remember whether I had kissed my brothers goodbye. I remembered telling them

Allah ﷻ would help, but I had been somewhat guarded. I smiled but had not further engaged. Our dinner the night before my operation was a blur. I was there but not present. A part of me came out a few minutes before the surgery at the hospital ward. I was just with my parents. I hugged them, joked with them, leaned my forehead against theirs, and glanced into their eyes with a grin. My brothers were away at school.

When it was time for my operation, the hospital staff pushed my bed down the ward. I held my mother's hand as she walked beside the bed. I smiled, trying my best to stay strong, but once separated from my parents and behind operating doors, the lights glared down at me, and the flood of guilt poured down.

I wanted to escape the operating room just like I had escaped from spending time with my brothers.

My heart ached as the needle pierced through my skin. The doctor found my vein and was now getting the anesthesia ready. I scrambled for time by asking Allah ﷻ for forgiveness. I requested Him to be Merciful to my parents and not take their daughter away. I wanted to spend time with my brothers and to be truly present. I yearned for comfort and clarity and wondered which Prophet's story would be of help for me at that time. I thought that maybe the story of Yūsuf ﷺ would come to mind since I was now separated from my family. It was, however, the story of Yūnus ﷺ that kept flooding through. I wondered why not the story of Mūsā ﷺ since he had to be brave and marched towards courage. How Allah ﷻ helped him escape from Pharaoh despite being trapped in front of the sea.

Will You help me make it to the other side?

I could not understand why the story of Yūnus 🕊 kept tugging at me.

Was it because he was trapped in a whale, and I was similarly trapped?

Is it a sign that—I too—will get out?

The moral of the story had to be more profound than that.

The anesthesia started to kick in. I did not have enough time. I talked to the doctors hoping that maybe I would feel alert for a little longer so I could reflect. As I started to slip into unconsciousness, I declared a promise to Allah 🕊.

The promise—if He let me—was to find out the relevance within the story of Yūnus 🕊.

'Inshā'Allāh, I will try to understand,' I mumbled within my head as the glaring operating room spun into pitch black.

Darkness was my company for the next eighteen hours.

The Story of Yūnus 🕊—the Path from Guilt to Forgiveness of the Self

I remember the last few minutes before I was flooded with light.

Doctors were telling my parents that I might be unconscious for a long time. I did not understand how I was able to know what was happening around me but was not able to open my eyes. I could hear nurses at a distance scribbling down what the doctors said on paper, and to my left, I could hear my father's shuffling steps. I tried to move but could not wiggle my fingers. I wanted to show them signs that I was there, but it felt like I was in the depths of the unknown—the only thing familiar was darkness.

I asked Allah ﷻ for help and gripped onto my promise for the story of Yūnus ﷺ.

'This is how Yūnus ﷺ must have felt in the belly of the whale,' I thought.

I did not know the prayer Yūnus ﷺ made when in the whale, but I told Allah ﷻ while trying to push my eyes open, that his prayer is the way I hope to call out to Him. I promised Allah ﷻ that I would look into his prayer and story in depth.

I promise.

Light flooded through.

I sat up the next day, and returned home three weeks later, to fulfill my promise by first looking at the prayer Yūnus ﷺ made.

His prayer and example can guide us to move away from guilt and towards forgiveness of the self.

Here are the steps to do so:

1. Embrace Regrets with Repentance

Allah ﷻ says,

*'[Yūnus] cried through **the depths of darkness** (saying): 'There is no God but You, **Glorified be You!** Truly, **I have been of the wrongdoers.**''*

(*al-Anbiyā'* 21: 87)

Yūnus ⚬ was in darkness from the depths of the night, sea, and whale. He was in darkness upon darkness, trapped, and helpless. He had regret and was in repentance.

Yūnus ⚬, as a Prophet, warned his people of a storm coming as a form of punishment if they disobeyed. The people of Yūnus ⚬ did not seem to take heed of his message, so he left his people out of frustration. When Yūnus ⚬ was within the whale after the storm, he regretted having left his people. He realized that he should not have been frustrated with them and should have assumed the best. The time spent avoiding his people was his time away from his responsibility as a Messenger.

This made me recall how I had been with my brothers. I chose to avoid them out of wanting to protect them. I was frustrated whenever they would insist on spending time with me. This was actually me avoiding my role as their elder sister: my duty to be fully present as opposed to avoiding them by playing games. This led to regret.

I repented to Allah ⚬ when I realized my shortcomings. I told Him that I needed to escape by keeping my mind busy before the operation and was unsure how to reassure my brothers without giving them false hope. I then acknowledged this was no excuse, but that I hoped to improve. I told Him I would quit gaming to spend more time with my brothers, and I asked Him to help me not get so easily frustrated whenever I felt the need to be alone. This is how I sought repentance.

The first step to moving from guilt to forgiveness of the self is to acknowledge our regrets with repentance. Acknowledge our shortcomings to Allah ﷻ through the realization of our mistakes.

2. CHANGE OF ACTIONS

Yūnus ﷺ felt regret for leaving his people. As soon as Allah ﷻ brought him out of the whale, he took time to rest, then he returned to his people. He did not wallow in regret. He showed Allah ﷻ his eagerness to learn from his guilt by returning, ready to fulfill his purpose.

The acknowledgment that I had been wrong—firstly to Allah ﷻ and later to my brothers—allowed me to forgive myself. I showed my apology to my brothers by returning to them with warmth. I chose to be the best sister that I could be. My brothers did not need to come to my room to ask if they could play because I would go to their room first. I stopped playing computer games and tried catching their tennis ball whenever they threw it. I was away from school, but whenever they would come home, I asked them about their day. I watched over them doing their homework and shared the short story that I had started to write. I talked to them about Allah ﷻ and the Prophets. *I was myself again.* I let them peek at the tip of my scar that started from my neck and let them marvel over how cool they found it. *Their sister had rods of steel infused within her spine.* It was fascinating to them that their sister did not squeal over blood, had a breathing machine that made her sound like Darth Vader, and was now like Superman or Ironman. I smiled at them, disagreeing whether I was more like Superman or Ironman, but what was clear—and a great honour for me—was that I was their sister.

I am so very proud of all siblings of those with disabilities for staying strong.

3. SEE THE GOOD THAT COMES FROM SHORTCOMINGS

Yūnus ﷵ returned to find his people listening attentively and understanding. He would not have valued this as much if he had not previously left in frustration. His time away was not a state of loss, but gain. He got to understand the beauty and wisdom in the plans of Allah ﷻ. He did more after repenting and learning from his shortcomings. He was able to move away from his guilt because he recognized the gains. He valued it, learned from it, and was better for it.

Personally, I felt guilty for not realizing this sooner, but maybe my operation—and reactions thereof—was a means to learn. I discovered what it truly means to be an elder sister. I may have not been fully present a few months before the operation—as my way to cope—but I should not beat myself up for it. It was not a state of loss but rather gain since I came out better.

We are meant to be polished from our mistakes.

We are not meant to feel shame.

Move away from guilt towards forgiveness of the self.

In her book *The Gifts of Imperfection,* Brené Brown states that guilt is 'often positive while shame [is] often destructive.'[1]

---

1   (Brown 2010, 41)

The reason for this is that when we are ashamed, we feel bad about *who* we are, but when we are guilty, we feel bad about *what we did*. It is more constructive to learn from what we did, build from our experiences, and see the good in it, than to drown in shame.

Allah ﷻ amazingly kept me alive through my operation. Despite feeling guilty over my behaviour towards my brothers, I grew to forgive myself. I repented to Allah ﷻ, strived to be the best sister I could be, and realized that this experience had been necessary for me to learn something new. My mistakes pushed me to be a better sister than I had been before.

Mistakes are not meant to drown us.

They are a means of growth.

4. DEMONSTRATE SELF-COMPASSION

It takes courage and strength to be compassionate towards ourselves. We are worthy of the mercy of Allah ﷻ as well as His forgiveness. We are worthy of being saved.

When referencing the example of Yūnus ﷺ, Allah ﷻ promises believers:

'*And thus We do deliver [save] the believers.*'
(al-Anbiyā' 21: 88)

This is a promise Allah ﷻ gives us whenever we make mistakes.

We are worthy of being saved, just like how Yūnus ﷺ was saved.

Allah ﷻ tells us why He saved Yūnus ﷺ:

'Had he not been of them who glorify Allah, he would have indeed remained inside its belly [the fish] till the Day of Resurrection.'
(al-Ṣāffāt 37: 143–144)

Yūnus ﷺ glorified Allah ﷻ after realizing his mistakes. He acknowledged that Allah ﷻ can do all things and is deserving of praise and gratitude.

As long as we repent, and give thanks and praise to Allah ﷻ, we are worthy of being saved.

We are worthy of answering the call to courage.

If we are worthy of being saved—are we not worthy of self-forgiveness?

Chapter 6

From Holder of Pain to Forgiver of Others

People with disabilities are generally excluded, belittled, and, at times, ostracized by some of their peers. This is due to the prevalence of ableism within the community. Ableism is the discrimination and social prejudice against people with disabilities and people who are perceived to be associated with a disability. People with invisible disabilities and their carers can also experience ableism. People with visible disabilities are, however, at a higher risk of facing more severe forms of ableism.

I have experienced feelings of ableism often, which only increased when I developed a more visible disability after using the wheelchair. I have learnt that in order to grow, I needed to let go of the pain and grant forgiveness. This process was an ongoing cycle due to the frequency of such painful experiences.

I will refer to one peer as Daisy. Her actions are a mere representation of the kind of encounters those with disabilities endure.

I messaged Daisy—as my sister in faith—to escort a newcomer to our community to my neighbourhood as the two sisters were nearby. Daisy and I were both involved in community volunteer work but I had only met her once. I noticed at our first brief encounter that she was talking to me in a belittling tone, but I assumed that it was her first time talking to a person with a disability and that she probably did not realize that her behaviour was condescending. I thought that if we all spent time together by being there for our new sister by introducing her to the marketplace and mosque nearby, Daisy might eventually feel comfortable around a person with a disability. I expressed to Daisy that she could bring along a friend, too. We set a date online—after I reconfirmed with my parents—for a few days after. We messaged each other good night while stating that we looked forward to seeing each other in a few days.

The next day my mom came home and asked if I was going out with my peers as planned because she had just seen them at the market but was not sure. I said it could not be true due to the confirmed date. I turned my laptop on to view their profiles, and indeed there were pictures of them at the marketplace. At that point, my father returned from the mosque and heard us talking about this. He comforted me and said that he saw them at the mosque, but was similarly not sure.

I felt hurt, not so much due to being excluded, but because my parents had witnessed it.

I messaged Daisy to give her the chance to explain. Open communication would provide room to build trust and clear potential misunderstandings. Daisy—instead of understanding why it was painful for me to have my parents witness this—brought her sister into the conversation who tried to intimidate me by typing in caps.

This inflicted more pain.

I read our conversation from the night before. I could not see how there could be room for any misunderstanding since a date and time had been clearly set. It was from that day I decided to avoid such company of peers. I decided to let go by not engaging further, deleting the messages, and busying myself with writing articles.

I assumed that my parents witnessing me being ostracized had happened for a good reason despite appearing terrible. Perhaps it was a means to protect me from trusting, or assuming that every peer with similar community-care interests is kind. It was painful, but it taught me that I should not trust people too easily—I should trust my first instincts more.

I could not always avoid community events, so I had to repeatedly go through the process of letting go of the pain and forgiving again.

When I arrived in the morning for a community event, Daisy came over first thing and asked why I was there and not at home instead. I was taken aback. Daisy quickly said, 'Due to your health.' She knew I was a university student and was aware that I spent all day at a lot of events, so why was she talking to me that way? Whenever I would ask why she was treating me this way, she would reply saying that I misunderstand her and only feel that way due to being 'disabled'.

I had to repeatedly forgive Daisy for the pain and for gaslighting me.

The term 'gaslighting' refers to the manipulative behaviour used to confuse people into thinking that their feelings—usually of pain—towards their experiences are off base. *How they misunderstand.* The effects of prolonged gaslighting make us question what is real, whether we are bad, and whether our minds are working properly. This is how confidence is stripped. This is how instincts are buried.

I went through periods of doubting my instincts and questioning whether I had truly forgiven Daisy. I did not hold anything against her and approached her as if nothing had happened. I kept in mind not to trust her unless she tried to regain my trust through inclusion. But every time a new hurtful action occurred, it felt like I was carrying the hurt she had given me before on top of the new pain that she was inflicting. The blows intensified, leading me to a degree of numbness.

I went through the process of letting go of the pain and forgiving...all over again.

The Understanding of Forgiveness—Key to Letting Go of the Pain

Forgiveness does not mean forgetting past pain when the same person hurts us again. I did not understand what forgiveness meant in depth. Because of that, I was confused about whether I had truly forgiven. It is natural to be reminded of past hurt when someone hurts us again. Ya'qūb ﷺ was brought back to the pain of losing Yūsuf ﷺ when he heard that his sons did not bring back home his youngest, Binyāmīn ﷺ.

> 'And he **turned away from them** and said, "Oh, **my sorrow over Yūsuf**," and his eyes became white from grief.'
>
> (*Yūsuf* 12: 84)

Ya'qūb ﷺ forgave by continuing to care for his sons, who had wronged Yūsuf ﷺ. He did not kick them out of their home. He did not obsess with proving his point after his sons tried to gaslight him by denying their wrongdoing. He told them he knew they were lying, but chose patience as his reaction, which allowed him to forgive.

Ya'qūb ﷺ said,

> 'No! Indeed your souls have tempted you to do something evil. So I can only endure with **beautiful patience**. It is from the help of Allah that I seek to bear your claims.'
>
> (*Yūsuf* 12: 18)

We have not forgiven someone if we repeatedly talk about their harm. It is normal to be triggered into remembering past actions when the same person hurts us again. This does not mean that we did not forgive them in the past. *It just means that we were pricked in a place that was already wounded.* It is natural for a continuous injury to be more tender and require more time to heal. We did not fail. We survived. We withstood. We are still persevering and need time to rise from the blow.

The key to letting go of pain is to understand what forgiveness means.

Forgiveness, according to *Merriam-Webster's Dictionary*, is to give up resentment towards the one that caused harm. Letting go of the resentment makes the pain go away. While resentment is carrying ill feelings towards someone or something that they did, forgiveness is letting go of those ill feelings. It is choosing not to retaliate and not wishing any harm to the person. It is wishing the best for their well-being and overall guidance. Forgiveness does not mean to freely trust someone who hurt us; nor does it mean to turn away from making them accountable. *We have the right to ask someone that harmed us to explain.*

I realized that I had forgiven Daisy after I chose to invest my time in pursuing my article-writing goals shortly after getting hurt. It is hard to focus on our goals and self-development when we have not forgiven someone, because our time is consumed with thinking about them or the harm they did. It is possible to feel pain because it is natural to need time to heal. I deleted those messages that were a reminder of my experience shortly after realizing that it was pointless to engage with her further. We need to practise self-compassion towards our growth.

Brené Brown says in *Rising Strong:*

'Forgiveness is **not forgetting** or **walking away from accountability** or condoning a hurtful act; it is the **process of taking back** and **healing our lives** so we can **truly live**.'[2]

Forgiveness is letting go of pain to *hold onto our responsibility towards growth*. The act of holding onto pain is letting go of our chance to grow. Those who hurt us do not deserve to be the reason

---

2   (Brown 2015, 151)

we delay our growth. With this in mind, we may be able to move past our pain faster and forgive.

The beautiful patience of Yaʿqūb ﷺ did not mean that he did not hold his sons accountable. Do not be overpowered by someone gaslighting the situation so that there is doubt about the reality that we experienced. Say that it is understood clearly, but if they deny, find the beauty in leaving the situation with beautiful patience.

Ibn Taymiyyah ﷺ was once asked about 'beautiful patience' (*ṣabr jamīl*), 'beautiful pardon' (*ṣafḥ jamīl*) and 'beautiful avoidance' (*hajr jamīl*). He answered that b*eautiful avoidance (hajr) is to **leave without harming (adah)**, beautiful pardoning is to **pardon without rebuking ('itab)**, and beautiful patience is to be **patient without complaining (shakwah)***.[3]

Steps in Letting Go of the Pain

Forgiveness is the key to letting go of pain, but how do we accurately unlock that key and make sure that we grow? How do we guarantee that we take every step needed to forgive wholeheartedly?

Below are steps to ensure that we thoroughly let go of pain and wholeheartedly forgive.

---

3   (Ibn Tayimiyyah 2016, 165)

1. Recognize that the Path of Attaining Internal Strength Requires us to Face Harm from Others

The attainment of internal strength is a painful road filled with thorns. Some are naturally placed, and others are purposefully placed by those who intend harm. Inner strength is a path where we endure and heal from pain. It is a chance to persevere and grow stronger. We become individuals of resilience who battled with revenge to choose forgiveness. We stand up to wrongful actions. We stand with compassion to encourage goodness. We face situations that are out of our control but direct every thought to what we can control. It is an act of courage and a form of patience. Pain does not become our identity. Strength becomes our identity. It is the strength within us that surfaces just when we are made to feel the weakest. It is through apparent weakness and grief that we take the responsibility to grow.

Grow with a vision in mind.

A goal.

Hope.

The hope that everything we are going through is needed for us to find strength from within.

The attainment of strength requires us to face harm from others. There is no other way to find out that we have this strength. Goodness from our core is unleashed when we are kind to those who harmed us. The way for us to truly stand is to have an unkind action to stand up to.

The only way for us to truly bloom is to endure all thorns.

Prophet Muhammad ﷺ forgave the people of Ṭā'if when they sent their children to throw rocks at him to drive him out of their city.

He wished good and forgave them by keeping his message—his vision—in mind.

He said,

*'I rather **hope** that Allah will raise, from **among their descendants, people** who will worship God as One and will not ascribe partners to Him.'*

(Bukhārī)[4]

Prophet Muhammad ﷺ had hope for the people. *Those who forgive wish good towards those who harm. They let go of their pain by keeping their vision in mind.* Prophet Muhammad ﷺ looked to the future and focused on his mission. He had a vision. He looked at the bigger picture.

Look at the bigger picture. Look at the vision. Focus on the mission. The legacy and imprint to leave behind a mark. Let the pain go. We can bring change by moving hearts and minds, out of the mercy of Allah ﷻ. Everything is in His Hands. Prophet Muhammad ﷺ attained the fruits of forgiveness by ending up to be the leader of Arabia, including Ṭā'if. Let go of the pain through forgiveness to attain the fruits of forbearance.

---

4   (Ṣaḥīḥ al-Bukhārī, 642)

2. Understand that those who Inflict Pain are Usually those who Hold Pain Themselves

Everyone has a backstory and hidden pain. Everyone may be trying to let go of that pain, and many may find it hard to do so. Some let go by inflicting pain towards others. Understanding the pain of others may help us let go of our pain and see that the pain that they inflict on us is not personal. Rather It is their struggle to attain internal strength. Do not accept their behaviour but empathize by letting go of the pain and by forgiving.

The first time someone of the same age hurt me was when I was four. I was excited to greet her at home for the first time, so I took out all my toys for her to play with. I happily stood to give some to her, but she did not respond nicely. She angrily asked why I was taller than her. Her tone confused me, and I did not understand why she was asking me that question instead of playing.

I realized when I had gone to her home that she did not have a lot of toys. I shared all my toys with good intentions, but I did not know that it hurt her since I had more toys in comparison. My presence hurt her, causing her to inflict pain upon me. It was neither nice nor fair, but it helped me to understand *why* she was hurting me. Understanding the reason made it easier to choose empathy and forgiveness over my pain.

Recognizing the background of others can help us develop the strength for compassion. This could aid in not inflicting pain in return. It could aid in forgiving.

One hadith relates:

*'Have **mercy on those on Earth**, and **the One in heaven will have mercy on you**.'*

(Abū Dāwūd)[5]

Assume that those who harm are holding onto sadness we do not know about.

It may be obvious someone is lying or intentionally harming us. It is best to show mercy by removing ourselves from that situation or keeping the pain of others in mind when talking to them about how their actions are hurtful.

The brothers of Yūsuf ﷺ hurt him, but it was due to their internal conflict of not knowing why their father favored him and Binyāmīn over them.

They said,

*'Truly, Yūsuf and his brother [Binyāmīn] are **more loved by our father than we**, but we are 'uṣbah (**a strong group**). Really, our father is in **plain error**.'*

(Yūsuf 12: 8)

The brothers felt insecure.

*'Verily, in Yūsuf and his brothers are **signs** (or symbols) for **seekers of Truth**.'*

(Yūsuf 12: 7)

---

5   (Sunan Abū Dāwūd 43, 169)

Understand the pain of others to be free from the pain they inflicted on you. Let us strive to be amongst those who not only forgive but also do good: *the muḥsinūn.*

3. GRIEVE THE LOSS OF EXPECTATIONS

We get hurt because we expect to be treated with kindness. I assumed Daisy was genuine when we agreed on a date to meet. I inadvertently had expectations of inclusion, and when that expectation was not met, it hurt.

We should all be kind and inclusive, but is it fair to set expectations for everyone when we all have the choice of how to be? It is not up to us to decide how a person behaves. We can let them know what we need, but in the end, they have the right to make that choice. We need to let go of our expectations to avoid disappointments. Expectations lead to disappointments, and disappointments lead to pain.

Brené Brown in *Rising Strong* says,

> '**Disappointments** *may be like paper cuts, but if those cuts are deep enough or if there are enough of them, they can* **leave us seriously wounded.**' [6]

When we avoid pain through disappointments, it will be easier to forgive. It is natural to expect someone not to be mean and feel upset at a loss over potential kindness. We need to grieve that loss

---

6   (Brown 2015, 141)

to move forward. We need to mourn and let go of reality of what? if we want to let go of the pain.

Let go of the relationship pictured; I pictured a sincere sisterhood with Daisy. I had to let that picture go. I had to let that relationship die and form a new one where I treated her more like an acquaintance. I could not afford to expect to be treated like a sister because that expectation led to hurt.

The shift in expectation ensures that we forgive them for the past. It paves the way for easier forgiveness if they end up harming again. It ensures we let go of pain to not only look after our emotional, mental, and physical well being, but also to give ourselves the chance to grieve. We need to allow ourselves to feel upset over loss since this is part of the human experience. Forgiveness means that we do not hold a grudge. We instead allow ourselves to grieve to come out better.

Brené Brown says in *Rising Strong,*

> 'We can't heal if we can't grieve; **we can't forgive if we can't grieve.** We run from grief because loss scares us, yet **our hearts reach towards grief because the broken parts want to mend.**'[7]

It is only when we grieve that we can truly mend; it is only when we mend that we can truly grow.

---

7 (Brown 2015, 138)

4. Focus on Being Our Best Selves by Wishing The Best for Others

The act of praying to Allah ﷻ when we are oppressed can liberate us.

As narrated in a hadith,

> 'Beware of the **supplication of the oppressed** for there is **no barrier between it and Allah.**'
>
> (Tirmidhī)[8]

I used to approach my contacts—including those who have harmed me—during the month of Ramadan to ask if they have any specific prayer requests. It was a way to shift my focus from the wrongs people do to what I can do. Even though I felt caged when around them with my voice silenced, the act of lifting my hands up in prayer for goodness towards them freed me. It melted my pain and helped me see that even though I was not treated as their sister, I could still behave like one to them. It is an act of strength to pray for goodness towards those who have harmed us.

Forgiveness is not just avoiding retaliation but going one step further and wishing good.

Allah ﷻ says,

> 'And not equal are the good deed and the bad. **Repel [evil] by that [deed] which is better,** and thereupon the one whom **between you and him is enmity [will become]** as though he was a devoted friend.'
>
> (Fuṣṣilat 41: 34)

---

8   (Tirmidhī 27, 120)

The act of praying for them instead of against them was an action *for* me, too. It was a means to earn the mercy of Allah ﷻ.

Allah ﷻ said about Prophet Muhammad ﷺ,

'It is due to the **mercy from Allah that you deal with them gently,** and had you been rough, **hard-hearted,** they would **certainly have dispersed** from around you. **Pardon them and ask pardon for them.**'

(Āl 'Imrān 3: 159)

Kindness through forgiveness—and asking forgiveness from God for those who harmed us—is a form of mercy from Allah ﷻ. We are not at a loss when harmed, wronged, belittled, or oppressed. We are amongst the strong. We are amongst those who have the strength to spread goodness, despite the harshness received from others.

The wrongs from others become insignificant when we shift our focus to the mercy of Allah ﷻ. Allah ﷻ helped Muhammad ﷺ rise with influence.

We might be wronged, but that is our chance to rise.

5. Focus on Marching Forward with the Door of Past Pain Shut

It is painful when people deny their actions and make others believe their untruths by using our background—our circumstances—against us. It is traumatizing when the oppressor plays the victim, especially when we have been enduring extensive harm at their hands. The flashbacks of what they did keep coming back because the pain we now experience is trauma. Let us forgive but do not keep worrying over whether we have truly forgiven. Close the chapter, even if unsure that we forgave. We need to live our lives, knowing that we tried our best. *Move forward.* This takes strength. We may have been treated unjustly in this world, but when we forgive, those who crossed the line multiple times will still have to answer back to the One who witnesses all. There will be a point where they will be held accountable whether in this life or the next.

This is why there is the Day of Judgement—a day of mercy for those wronged and oppressed.

6. Heal by Allowing the Sincere to Comfort and Lift

I realized that not talking to my parents regarding any future experiences with Daisy made it harder for me to see why I was treated this way. It is harder to heal when we do not understand why pain is inflicted upon us and when we try to figure out the pain caused by others on our own. It was only after talking to my parents that my initial instincts regarding Daisy were confirmed, and that anyone treated that way would also feel pain. There were times when I found it hard to bring it up to my parents because I did not want them to know of the dragging-down behaviour of some peers towards their child; during these times I found comfort from my husband, siblings, and sincere sister-friends. They lifted me up whenever they noticed that I was treated in a derogatory manner by some of my peers—they helped me go through the process of openly talking to my parents which promoted my healing process.

We strive to follow the footsteps of the Prophets, but in the end, we can never have the strength they had nor the comfort they received. We find hope and direction, but there will come a time when we will need more help than hope. *We will need support.* We try everything, only to go through the repetitive cycle of being hurt, letting go of the pain, and forgiving.

Accept help so we can break free from having to go through the same cycle again.

**

Forgiveness by letting go of pain was never meant to be easy. It is challenging to live in a world, knowing that we were wronged while seeing the person who hurt us pretend as if they did right. It is hard to check whether we truly forgave. I got to understand how truly hard it is to forgive continuously after reading about a Companion from Madinah during the time of Muhammad ﷺ. He was promised the highest level of Paradise due to his nightly habit of forgiving those who harmed him.[9] The fact that he did so every night before he went to sleep made me wonder if someone new hurt him every day. I have grown to realize that we might keep forgiving the same person over and over again for the same action, due to them pretending as if everything is okay.

Traumas are usually remembered before we fall asleep.

Let go of pain and forgive before sleeping to attain the highest level of Paradise. It is hard, but it is through this hardship that we will find strength from within.

---

9   (Musnad Aḥmad, 12286)

We rise by letting go of pain and forgiving. We are not defeated for getting harmed. We are not weak for experiencing pain. We are not worthless for not being heard. We are gathering up the strength to stand and rise. Rise towards goodness. Rise with grace. Rise in having the courage to encourage someone inflicting pain to stop. Act out of wanting the best for them with forgiveness instead of revenge.

As Brené Brown said in *Rising Strong,*

> '*The **brokenhearted** are indeed the **bravest among us**—they **dared to love** and they **dared to forgive**.*' [10]

O braveheart, let us dare ourselves to let go of pain and forgive.

---

10 (Brown 2015, 156)

Chapter 7

From Guarded to Approachable

I wholeheartedly forgave, but I built walls. This was the only way to cope and navigate the world around me, because keeping my heart on my sleeves only led to heartbreak and hurt, causing me to blame myself for not having remained guarded.

This was a lifestyle that I unintentionally chose.

I was not aware that I had been guarded until a new classmate in high school pointed it out.

I missed out half of my second-to-last year of high school due to illnesses. I restarted midway by joining the grade below me. I returned as the new girl. This was an identity that was different—and separate—from my identity as someone with a disability.

My first class back was in English literature. I smiled and greeted everyone at my table and sat down, gripping my sleeves.

'It's nice to meet all of you. I am Sa'diyya,' I said, beaming, not knowing whether to keep looking at their faces or look down. I opened my files and wrote while occasionally looking up to smile at those around me.

One of my new classmates chuckled to herself while muttering something that I could not make out.

'Sorry I did not hear,' I said in an attempt to engage.

'How can you be kind yet so guarded?' She shrugged as she leaned forward. *'You can tell you are kind...but you are too guarded.'*

I did not know how to reply.

I was not aware that I appeared kind and did not know that I was guarded. Those around her apologized on her behalf and explained that she tends to say what is within her heart. I beamed, saying it was refreshing to hear such honesty.

'I did not know that I was guarded,' I mustered the strength to reply. *'And I do not know why I am guarded either. Maybe we can get to know each other, and you can help me figure it out?'* I smiled with a shrug.

She returned a smile, saying that she would love to. From there she became my friend—Moeka.

An hour later, it was the end of class, and the teacher lifted me up from my chair. My new classmates watched, alarmed. They did not know that I had a disability. I did walk differently, but it was not apparent at first glance. Moeka rushed to stand up and asked if she could walk with me down the corridor.

I jokingly warned that I was a slow walker.

'*Good,*' she grinned. '*A chance for me to get to know you better.*'

We walked into the crowded corridor. I used my arms as a shield to step forward and make sure that I did not fall. It was my coping mechanism to navigate amidst the crowd. I tried to talk, but I was too focused on walking. I worried about how to let Moeka know, but I think she realized that it was hard to fully engage.

'*You are guarded **because** you are kind,*' she exclaimed.

I could tell that she had more to say.

'*You got hurt and forgave too many times—this is why you are guarded. Your kindness made you guarded,*' she muttered.

I smiled as she tried to figure me out. I told her that she might be right. I expressed that I would try to figure out how to be kind and not guarded at the same time. I wanted to discover how to wear my heart on my sleeve and not get hurt. I wanted to understand how to keep moving forward without holding back.

When we reached the end of the corridor, she raised her arms out for a hug. I loosened my arms. I was afraid to fall amidst the crowd, but I let her hug me, and I wrapped my arms around her.

I let her in.

'You tell me when you figure out how to be kind, and not guarded at the same time, because I get hurt a lot too.' She smiled.

'I will,' I said as I wondered how I could feel so close to someone I barely knew.

Later during the day, just as I was about to pass through a door, I reached out to hold it open for some students who were connecting to another building. Every time I thought I would take the leap and move, someone new kept passing by. Standing there, I wondered how I could be guarded despite wanting to be there for others. Some old classmates that passed through knew of my disability, but a lot of them did not take a second glance to greet me. My arms started to wobble, but more people from my previous year passed by. I smiled, thinking that one of them would hold the door. There were a few that smiled, but they glided past the door without a second thought.

'It's hard to be kind,' I thought as the inside of me numbed.

Numbness shielded me from pain—it protected me from the break.

I stopped expecting from people and turned to Allah ﷻ. I asked if there was anyone amongst the crowd to help hold the door. I wondered if there was anyone brave enough to be kind—anyone strong enough to be a warrior sent by God.

The crowd decreased until I heard one person in the distance. I was about to walk through but realized that the one left was a younger teen with Down's syndrome. I stayed back to hold the door because I thought, out of everyone, he deserved it.

He stood before me and was about to pass, but when he saw me, he held out his hand and gently pulled back the other side of the two-sided door. He gestured with his other hand that I move forward. I did not let go of the door handle because I wanted to show him that I was holding the door for him to pass instead. The more I indicated that I was holding the door for him, the more he revealed that he was there to hold the other door for me. I was moved. Admiration and gratitude overflowed—a sharp contrast from numbness.

I looked into his eyes and said 'thank you' from the bottom of my heart as he gave me permission to move forward. I did not expect to be approached with beautiful kindness. Before passing through the doorway, I stood humbled in recognition of the person placed before me.

A warrior sent by God.

I grinned, walking down the empty corridor that echoed my footsteps. I was beaming over witnessing the beauty of kindness and experiencing it firsthand. Allah ﷻ chose to reply. He picked someone from the crowd, and the one He picked was a form of reassurance. It was a reminder to always approach people with kindness, regardless of our circumstances. It may be hard, but by doing so, we can be amongst the strong. We can be chosen as warriors sent by God.

What I learned—from the warrior God sent that day—regarding kindness without being guarded were the following:

1. Being Sure of Who We are and the Kindness that We want to Spread

The warrior sent by God was so sure of who he was and how he wanted to help hold the door open. This was how he wanted to offer his help at that moment because this was part of his identity, his essence. It did not matter that someone else held the door open for him because he was so sure that he wanted to hold the door open for them. He wanted to do that act of kindness, no matter what.

This taught me that no matter how people treat me, I should never stop being kind. The behaviour of others should not affect who I am. I can choose to stay away from those who harm me, but that does not mean that I change my actions when in their presence. It does not mean that I numb my emotions. I should dare myself to be there fully—and wholeheartedly—no matter how scary it is.

Prophet Muhammad ﷺ did not change his behaviour towards some of the Makkans who spread false rumours about him. This was because he, as As-Ṣādiq—the truthful one—knew who he was and had the focus of spreading kindness.

What matters is knowing who we are and what we stand for. We need to own the part of ourselves that is kind without shaming ourselves or feeling weak.

Kindness is strength.

2. HABITUAL ACTIONS LEAD TO HABITUAL BEHAVIOURS

It was clear: the warrior sent by God acted out of habit. He did not think whether he should hold the door. *He just did.* This showed that whenever it comes to kindness, do not think, but do. The more we do—without analyzing—the easier it will be to remain kind, despite how those around us act.

It is not possible to be guarded when it is our habit to approach people with kindness. It might be hard to habitually perform acts of kindness, but strength will emerge with kindness as our habitual behaviour.

Prophet Mūsā ﷺ was in extreme difficulty when he was in the desert after escaping Pharaoh. He refers to himself as *faqīr*—someone in a state of weakness and helplessness out of need—when praying to Allah ﷻ during this moment of his life. This, however, did not stop Mūsā ﷺ from helping the daughters of Shuʿayb ﷺ to collect water from the well in order to protect them from men who were harassing them. This shows how habitual acts of kindness beget strength even in times of difficulties.

3. THE BREAKING OF OUR SHELLS LETS HUMANITY OUT

I thought that I ought to be kinder to the teen with Down's syndrome, above any of my other peers. It was wrong to distinguish him due to his exterior. I should have been kind without categorizing him. He was like everyone else, and was someone worthy of recognition, due to his interior. He was a warrior sent by God because of his kind heart. His disability was not the reason why he was chosen, but his ability to be kind, and his ability to be human.

There must have been many who judged him or treated him differently. He must have felt it. *I know what that is like.* What we feel can crack us open. No number of walls can prevent the shell within us from cracking. *We are human.* There is no running from the reality of how we feel. No amount of numbing can guarantee that we will remain numb. We will feel that prick from the thorn. We may be able to keep some people away, but it will not stop them from shooting arrows from the other side of the wall. Guardedness is not the solution. *It is a barrier.* A barrier to letting out our humanity wholeheartedly.

Walls prevent us from being fully present.

Prophet Muhammad ﷺ was loved not only by Muslim believers but those of different faiths, too. This was because of how his humanity was felt through his being wholeheartedly present with kindness.

Use his example: be wholeheartedly present, without any barriers. It is the best way to show our humanity.

Lack of kindness may be the norm due to today's 'survival-of-the-fittest' society. This mentality makes it challenging to do acts of kindness, despite kindness being our core quality. It may be the reason why we do not break our shells to let our humanity out. It is easier to cover up our cores and put up a front as an act of survival. It is easier to numb ourselves and not be wholeheartedly present. It is easier to not be fully awake. This is because kindness is scarce with guardedness—and meanness—on the rise.

The understanding of this norm led me to understand who I *do not* want to be. I did not want to be vague; I wanted to be transparent. I did not want to be cold; I wanted to be warm. I did not want to bottle up my feelings; I wanted to be authentic.

I wanted to find strength by following the way of the Prophets.

People would not be able to understand my roots if I did not sprout out from the ground.

I want the people I meet to connect with my roots by knowing who I am.

How would they know if I do not break through the cracks?

Be real and transparent. Be fully present despite the climate. This will ensure we remain grounded and display our humanity wholeheartedly throughout the process. Realize that there is strength in showing up as our true authentic selves.

We deserve to show up from our seed's core into the world.

**

People might intentionally want to harm us when we show up from our core into the world. We may not be given a safe environment for that chance or space.

It is hard to be fully unguarded in a toxic scenario—we need some sort of shield.

Brené Brown wrote in *Rising Strong*,

*'Compassionate people are **boundaried people**.'* [11]

Compassion includes consideration for ourselves.

Brené Brown goes further to write,

> *'Compassionate people **ask for what they need**. They say no when they need to, and when they say yes, they mean it. They're **compassionate because their boundaries keep them out of resentment**.'* [12]

Be approachable, kind, and unguarded while ensuring self-preservation. Set boundaries and a tone to what kind of friendship is expected on both sides. Let us strive to be a friend who helps, but don't forget to help ourselves in the process. Be a person who forgives, but choose to trust only when someone earns your trust.

We should always set boundaries by telling people what we need and how we expect to be treated. Avoid company both in private and in a community setting if such standards are not met. Standards are also set based on how we behave and what we choose not to say. Real friends recognize that I pull away to help them grow. They do not get upset but rather respect the process by working towards growth. Our relationship is centered on mutual understanding. We are transparent with whatever makes us comfortable. We are aware of how to protect the friendship moving forward.

I am open to readjusting my boundaries if the other party displays growth. Still, if they do not, I only talk about work or

---

11 (Brown 2015, 114)

12 (Brown 2015, 115)

anything that is of relevance. I am myself in personality, but I do not share my life—and my world—with them. I give advice with full sincerity if they ask, but I do not share my struggles. I forgive, acknowledge their existence, and respect them as humans—I just do not hold them close to my heart.

Prophet Muhammad ﷺ was hurt by Hind before her conversion to Islam due to her mutilating his uncle's body after the Battle of Uhud. Hind became a completely different person after embracing Islam and became ashamed of her actions. However, there was the predicament of whether she should see the Prophet after her conversion. It was not out of assuming that there might be anger towards her past actions, but rather not wanting to remind him of the hurt from the memory of the pain.

Not everyone is meant to be part of our lives, just as not everyone was meant to be on the ark of Nūḥ ﷺ.

There is always the risk of drowning if we let everyone in.

Chapter 8

From Caged-in to Unlocking of Potential

When I was young, there were a lot of sports competitions in my school. I assumed that we are all meant to discover a sport that brings out our strengths to discover our potential. I thought, *there must be one sport that I can do.* Call it wishful thinking, but with the help of my father, I tried swimming, hitting a tennis ball, and riding a bike. I could hardly do a lap in the pool, barely hit the tennis ball once, and riding a bike with trainers only got harder with time. I could not surpass other children, but I thought maybe I could surpass my own record in due course. But I only got worse. It was futile to proceed.

Every child chooses a sport. I was the only one who did not discover what I could do. I was meant to grow, but I did not know how. I was introduced to creative arts but thought that the basics of arts meant drawing. I drew, but nothing I pictured came to light. I was given crafts when admitted to the hospital, so after book-reading, I drew. It required too much effort to colour inside the lines, let alone draw from imagination. I thought with time, I might get better.

As a ten-year-old, I packed colouring supplies when visiting Pakistan to see my grandparents and relatives. I thought that there would be places that I could not go to or activities that I could not do, so I would spend my time drawing. I stayed indoors with my supplies when my younger brothers were out with our cousins. On one such day, my grandfather was heading out to the library and asked if there were any books I wanted to borrow. He left to fetch some books as I continued with my drawing. I thought it would be easiest to draw the Kaaba because the main structure is a cube. I used the ruler and carefully measured each line before making any marks. I ended up using the rubber more than the pencil, and before I knew it, my grandfather had returned with some books.

'*What are you drawing?*' My grandfather from behind my seated chair.

I shyly covered the paper on the table that lay beneath my hand.

'*The Kaaba, but...it does not matter since I cannot draw.*'

He leaned over my shoulder and moved my hand to the side. He smiled and sat down with the books. I recognized one of the books that he had brought—titled *A True Friend of Children*—on Prophet Muhammad ﷺ. I had previously read it. I narrated my experience of reading it for the first time, what moved me, and the lessons I learned from it. I told him that when first reading it, I wondered whether Muhammad ﷺ would accept me and later discovered that he was a true friend of every child. He was a true friend, especially to those with disabilities. I told my grandfather how that book made me cry. The part where the beard of Prophet Muhammad ﷺ was soaked in tears after discovering baby girls buried alive. I expressed that girls in pre-Islamic Arabia were unwanted. They were considered weak, so I thought if I had been alive during that time, I would have been considered the weakest of all. My grandfather smiled with tears in his eyes.

'Prophet Muhammad ﷺ would have been your friend.'

I smiled, trying to hold back my tears. I was humbled, honoured, and overwhelmed. *How can I miss and love someone that I never met?* My grandfather told me that part of the book made him cry, too. That moment was when I first discovered the serenity of sharing experiences.

Later, during my stay, as I was attempting to climb the stairs with the help of my grandfather, I got frustrated and said that I could not do anything. I could not play sports nor properly draw. Everything that I tried ended in me failing miserably. I only got worse.

My grandfather pushed open the door at the front of the final few steps for us to enter his home.

'There are some doors only you can unlock and push open.'

I was puzzled by my grandfather's reply. Everything requires some sort of physical activity, including the unlocking and pushing of doors. I knew there was a deeper meaning that I would only understand with time.

'*Allah* 🕮 *has special plans for everyone, including you,*' my grandfather continued as he pulled me up the last step.

We had entered our home, but I felt lost. *What special plans?* I did not see what my grandfather saw, but I believed he was telling the truth. I knew that Allah 🕮 has special plans for everyone, including me, but I did not wholeheartedly believe the extent of such plans being special for me.

'*Always remember what Grandfather said,*' I thought.

When my three-week stay with my grandfather and relatives was over, my family and I flew back home, and I resumed my last year of primary school. Towards the last week of school, I sat in the back of the bus with my classmate, talking about the day that we had just spent together. She lay down on the empty seat and told me to continue talking about our day together.

'*Why? You know what happened,*' I blurted.

She smiled with her eyes closed.

'*You pick up the little things and narrate in a way that teaches me something new.*'

I was confused. I was just recounting our day as it had happened. What I noticed and how it made me happy. I did not see what there was to learn. I did not know that I narrated things or that I had a way of sharing.

She quickly got up and said, *'You make an ordinary day sound interesting. I saw what you saw, but through your eyes, I notice more,'* she said as she lay back down.

So, I began from the beginning and continued to the end. I mentioned how we came across each other while I was trying to go down the stairs, and it lifted me up. I told her that I valued her greeting me the way she did and how little things make a difference. I said that I found it funny when she told a joke in front of our other classmate, who did not get the joke. *I found that more hilarious than the joke itself.* I shared the moment during assembly when the teachers lowered their guards by having fun with the students. They were like friends, and that was something we needed. Why don't teachers come to play with us during lunchtime and only come for duty? The importance of maintaining authority but also leaving an impacting bond as humans. The importance of adults being friends to children. I stopped talking. I was beginning to notice what my friend meant, how I was narrating. I was sharing my internal reaction to our external experience. And I saw my friend's reactions to my narration: she chuckled at her joke as if she were hearing it for the first time; she pondered over my reaction to the teachers' actions during assembly; she smiled when I told her how she made me happy and how little gestures matter. I got to experience her realizing aspects of her day that she had previously not picked up on. Pointing them out made her see and feel the same experiences on a different level.

The serenity of sharing experiences.

When it was her time to get off the bus, she got up for a hug and whispered, 'Thank you.'

That day, I further realized how I internalize experiences and the serenity in sharing those experiences. This was not something a lot of people do. People mostly just live. I live and later relive to find something to value and learn. I also get to *see* the day, while most generally move around so much that they miss picking up the little things. My limited movement, due to my disability, enhanced my experiences. This is how I pick up details and how I remember them.

My grandfather once wrote to me before I started secondary school telling me how I had potential and that Allah ﷻ, as al-Walī—the Protecting Friend—would arrange a friend for me in every sphere of life.

Al-Walī had special plans for everyone, including me.

I did believe that al-Walī always arranges someone when we most need it, especially after reading the story of Prophet Ibrāhīm ﷺ.

Allah ﷻ gave Ibrāhīm ﷺ the noble title of *khalīlullāh* which means 'friend of Allah'.

Some from the village of Prophet Ibrāhīm ﷺ threw him in the fire, but al-Walī protected him from getting burnt.

It is clear throughout the stories of the Prophets that Allah ﷻ is a Protecting Friend to His creation and that there is potential for us all to work towards being accepted by Him—as long as we search for His signs, just like Prophet Ibrāhīm ﷺ did.

The recognition that Allah ﷻ, as al-Walī, sends people in every sphere of our lives, can help us eventually see our potential.

The reason for this is because we recognize their ability to aid our growth.

When I read my grandfather's letter, I could see how al-Walī sent my friend Salma to be my companion throughout primary school. The new friend that al-Walī chose for me throughout my secondary school experience was Mrs Alexander, who felt more like a friend than a teacher.

Through Mrs Alexander, the signs that Allah ﷻ had special plans for me were becoming clear, and I began to see that in my writing. Through writing short stories and blog posts, I recognized that narrating whatever I internalized was my path, and cultivating that skill was the key to unlocking my potential.

I got into Hong Kong University despite missing a lot of school and facing discouragements to apply. Allah ﷻ sent more special souls—like Mrs Alexander—along the way to help me. Their belief in my potential made me exert all my efforts towards that goal. My Uncle Jalal and his family helped me throughout the university application process, which strengthened me before sitting for my final exams. Imam Sulaiman and his wife—who were also from the Chinese Muslim community in Hong Kong—encouraged me to keep on trying. I also had Aunty Aisha as my live-in caretaker for the eight years of secondary school and university. She came the year my grandfather passed away when I was in my second year of secondary school. Aunty left her hometown in the Philippines to earn money for her daughter's operation, but her daughter passed away before she could save up. She discovered Islam at that period of grief. She embraced Islam and came across my family to find that I was about to go through the same operation her daughter had been scheduled for. Aunty Aisha took care of me like her daughter, loved me, encouraged me, stood up for me, and felt thrilled with anything that I achieved. She repeatedly reminded me of my grandfather's words: *'Allah ﷻ has special plans for everyone, including you.'*

The signs of Allah ﷻ are true.

Muslim students from earlier batches at my university tried to establish a Muslim Students' Association (MSA) but halted due to things not moving forward. Until that point, my whole life had been about discovering and unlocking potential. I wondered if my purpose—as someone in an electric wheelchair—was to say that I believe there was potential and that things were possible. *We should not give up on the MSA but keep moving forward.*

We are placed at particular doors to unlock and push them open. Our batch of students tried again to unlock the door, and we were successful; we were able to formally establish the MSA under the student union.

The signs of Allah ﷻ are true.

My mother helping me on campus during university allowed me to do extra-curricular community work. For the first time, I came across peers who converted to Islam, those who wanted to follow in the footsteps of the Prophets. They saw the Islam that I could see, Islam as it is meant to be, as our Prophets taught it to us. They could see how Allah ﷻ arranged companions for the Prophets, from Ādam ﷺ to Muhammad ﷺ, to help them in every sphere of their lives. They recognized this as one of the signs of Allah ﷻ for us to hold onto for our lives. They kept strengthening me. These Muslims who converted—which includes my husband—reminded me of my purpose. They made sure that I voiced my opinions. I knew when the imam and his wife came with my husband's proposal, that Allah ﷻ had prepared my husband as a friend for all spheres of my life.

The signs of Allah ﷻ are true.

When I was a little younger, I came across talks by Abu Hafsah Abdul Malik Clare, a visually blind brother. I asked him through commenting on his posts online how he was able to share his knowledge and experiences while having a disability since people judge us. He mentioned the importance of mentorship and surrounding ourselves with a strong support system.

I found that support system through writing.

Aunty Atiya was the first writer I came across in person who encouraged me to write and gave me critical feedback. I was later accepted into the SISTERs magazine family, founded by Sister Na'ima B Robert, and there I felt most at home. The network of writers in the magazine was the first place where sister-writers welcomed me, encouraged me, and noticed a side of me that I had not seen before. They showed me that my prose was poetic, that I could write poetry. The first adult book that was written by a Muslim sister that impacted me had been given to me by my sister-friend—Sarah—when I was sixteen years old. It was *'From My Sisters' Lips'* by Sister Na'ima B Robert. I had no idea that, in the future, I would be part of the SISTERs magazine family that she founded. I did not plan nor think that this would be my path, but it kept appearing to be so.

Allah ﷻ sends signs throughout our lives. *People throughout our lives.* He implanted the promise to write a book within my heart and had me remember it. At times, I doubted that I could fulfill that promise, but Allah ﷻ kept sending help.

A lot of us may not see the potential that we have. We may not wholeheartedly believe despite believing in God. He gives gifts to everyone, but there is hesitancy in accepting that He gave a gift to us, too. We question: What is out there that we can do? How can we be amongst those who make a positive difference? Are we worthy of doing so?

We are nothing in relation to Allah ﷻ. Still, in relation to people, we are all worthy of giving something back, even if we are paralyzed. Those who cannot move also have something to offer. I rather think they have *more* to give: they value little things in life that others would never be able to recognize.

We all have a purpose, a message to share. We need to believe that we are worthy of growth, worthy of the bloom.

Believe me, the signs of Allah ﷻ are true.

Steps in Discovering and Unlocking our Potential

1. Believe That Allah ﷻ Made Us All Capable of Something.

My mother introduced me to Helen Keller, a person who was both visually and hearing impaired, when I was hospitalized as a child. Helen learned the English language, despite neither hearing nor seeing. She had potential despite her limitations. *Everyone has potential.* I was holding some coins at the time and placed them in my mother's hands and closed my eyes. I clasped her hands shut and tried to put my fingers in between hers to feel the coins beneath her fingers. I tried to distinguish the coins that she was holding without seeing them. This soon developed into a game my mother and I would play during my hospital stays.

'Allah ﷻ has special plans for everyone, including you.' My mother spoke words that her father would later echo.

Allah ﷻ has special plans for everyone. He made us all capable of doing something.

Allah ﷻ says,

*'Indeed We **created man** from a drop of mingled sperm, to **test him**, and so We **gave him (the gifts)** of **hearing and sight.'***
(al-Insān 76: 2)

During university, I took a history course on autobiographies. One of the books included Helen Keller's autobiography titled *The Story of My Life.* I was thrilled to see how Helen captured language so beautifully and could 'see' and 'hear' what most could not. She wrote how her 'hands were busy listening' to gain knowledge of the world. She narrated her experiences of not physically seeing or hearing, due to being born with a disability, but how she had a 'sixth sense—a soul sense—which sees, hears, feels, all in one.' She states how her 'mind can see them all.' She was capable because Allah ﷻ made her capable.

We are all capable of the rise. It is a matter of recognizing the gifts of 'hearing' and 'sight' that God has given us.

As Allah ﷻ says,

'Did you imagine that We created you without any purpose?'
(al-Mu'minūn 23: 115)

Trust that Allah ﷻ will give us success whenever we unlock our potential. We might stumble and fail at first, but in the grand scheme of things, there will be success.

Allah ﷻ redirects us to say,

*'My **success can only come from Allah**, that **in Him I trust**, and **to Him, I will return**.'*
(Hūd 11: 88)

Utter these words. Allah ﷻ will help. Whatever we unlock within ourselves was meant for us to unlock, so that we may return to Him with a bloom.

This is the promise of Allah ﷻ.

*'The **promise of Allah is true**, but most of them do not know.'*
(al-Qaṣaṣ 28: 13)

2. RECOGNIZE YOUR VISION WITH PRAYERS.

The promises of Allah ﷻ are true.

As a child, my vision of writing a book was not clear. It was, nonetheless, a vision. I had the hope of sharing my experiences to lift my audience simply because other authors had lifted me during my time of need. I had made a promise to write a book, but I didn't know the kind of truths my life would entail, whether whatever I shared would be helpful or if I was dreaming too big. Whether I had made that promise out of frustration. How was I to know in which direction to go?

Allah ﷻ kept redirecting me to that promise because I had communicated that vision to none but Him.

'What is the point of the Prophets going through all that pain and hardship?' I had mumbled as a ten-year-old in confusion.

'Why was Prophet Yūsuf ﷺ shown that beautiful dream as a child, only to suffer later and be separated from his father?' I was back to asking the same questions two years after making my promise.

'Why does Allah ﷻ reply to me but also put me through hardship? I don't understand.'

I fumbled.

A few days after asking myself those questions, the teachers at my secular school introduced a school production on the story of Yūsuf ﷺ—*Joseph and the Technicolored Dreamcoat*. They told me how I would be one of the many narrators.

Goosebumps.

I did not expect Allah ﷺ to reply like...that.

I stood in line behind my classmates to ask our teacher why we were doing this specific play.

'It's a beautiful play. You will like it, Sa'diyya.'

I nodded with a smile and thanked her. I left the line, but shortly after that, I had other questions. I stood behind my classmates until it was my turn. This time I asked if there was a main lesson in the story.

'*It's a creative play to enjoy. Do not worry about learning a lesson from it. Just learn your lines as the narrator, and that is it.*'

I thanked her again with a smile, but after leaving the line, I felt the heaviness to ask something more. I returned and stood in line again until it was my turn. I asked if I had to be the narrator. I expressed that I did not mind being one of the slaves in Egypt, or the sun, moon, or one of the stars.

My teacher swiveled her chair closer to me and looked at me warmly with a smile.

'*Are you worried about learning the lines, Sa'diyya?*'

How could I tell her that I had questioned Allah ﷻ just a few days before about the story of Yūsuf ﷺ? Only to be told by a secular school that we are doing a play on that exact story? It felt like there was this big lesson right in front of me, but I was not ready to face it.

I was not worried about my lines; I was worried about not being able to learn the lessons God intended me to learn.

My teacher leaned forward.

'*The other roles require more physical activity. You can do this. There will be months of practice. Do you have any other questions?*'

I did not know what to say. I pointed toward the corner dedicated to practising our lines and said I would go over there and begin.

'*Thank you,*' I said while walking off.

'*Months of practice,*' I mumbled to myself.

Every Tuesday after school was rehearsal time. I felt frustrated about not understanding the answers to my questions. I rested during rehearsal one day and watched everyone perform, from the beginning until the end. As an observer, I saw how it was only possible for Yūsuf ﷺ to reach a prestigious position in Egypt—as opposed to the land he was from with his family—due to it being a developed civilization. He had to be separated from his family to grow. I still did not understand why, through a separation, there was growth. His dreams—his vision—shown at the beginning of the story, before his hardship, was a comforting reminder not to give up hope.

The main lesson is hope.

The hope that could be attained through our vision and prayer.

Allah ﷻ says,

'*And to **your Lord** alone, **turn** all your **intentions** and **hopes**.*'
(*al-Sharḥ* 94: 8)

When we think about our dreams—and the possibility of doing good—we naturally develop the feeling of hope, even if we are going through hardship.

Brené Brown said in her book *The Gifts of Imperfections,* that hope is not an emotion, rather:

'a way of thinking or a cognitive process.'[13]

We develop our thought processes by forming goals. We create steps to achieve such goals. This guides us to strengthen our hope. We are not powerless in developing hope since the development of hope is a 'learned process'. It is strengthened if we keep our goals in focus with perseverance.

As a child, I did not know how to fulfill my promise due to not having formative goals. I was too young.

It became more possible for me to develop hope when I was old enough to know how to set goals by forming intentions through prayer.

Allah ﷻ will make the steps clear.

'And He *found you lost* and *guided you.*'
(al-Ḍuḥā 93: 7)

The moment we recognize the signs of Allah ﷻ, we should pray with intention and humility, so that He may help us live out our vision with grace.

Allah ﷻ encourages us to pray,

'My Lord! *Lead me in with the Truth,* and *lead me out with the Truth,* and *grant me the strength to help me.*'
(al-Isrā' 17: 80)

---

13 (Brown 2010, 65)

Allah ﷻ shall grant us the strength to live out our dreams. He will lead us to the truth if we seek His help like those in history.

He always does.

I promise.

3. DARE TO LIVE BY EXERCISING YOUR SKILLS.

It was narrated in a hadith that,

> 'The **best food a man could eat** is what is **earned by him,** and the Prophet of God—**Dāwūd** ﷺ—ate from what **he earned from his hard work.** "
>
> (Bukhārī)[14]

Dāwūd ﷺ acted out his skill to not just survive, but to discover his potential. We feel more fulfilled earning from our hard work, passions, talents, and gifts.

This is what makes someone a person of strength—a person who dares to put themselves out there and live based on their God-given gifts and abilities.

Allah ﷻ describes Dāwūd ﷺ as saying,

> 'Our slave **Dāwūd, the man of strength,** ever **turned to his Lord.** '
>
> (Ṣād 38: 17)

---

14 (Ṣaḥīḥ al-Bukhārī, 2072)

A 'man of strength' means strength in devotion and doing good. It means *action*. Allah ﷻ refers to this concept of 'strength through action' for several Prophets.

Allah ﷻ says,

> *'And mention our slaves Ibrāhīm, Isḥāq, and Yaʿqūb, they **were owners of strength** (in worship and **righteous deeds**) and were **men of vision**. Surely, We conferred upon them **a special distinction** that they **remember the Hereafter**. And they are with Us, **verily of the chosen**, and the best.'*
>
> (*Ṣād* 38: 45–47)

The owners of strength are those who act in doing good. This is how they find their special plans. This is how a distinction emerges. This is how we unlock ourselves and rise.

4. Strengthen Your Drive by Helping Others, Especially Those You Love.

Mūsā ﷺ loved his people. He wanted them free. He was hesitant in speech, but his drive to help gave him additional strength.

I find it difficult to sit for long periods. But for me to write, I must sit. I overcome my hesitancy of staying seated for long stretches by remembering my vision. I keep in mind the potential good in my writing—and, consequently, those long periods of sitting—could bring, especially to those that I love. The joy in my parents' eyes is my drive to keep trying and discovering new genres to master. Narrating is not only writing prose; it is also writing scripts for giving talks. I continue to explore different ways to lift others through words. *Different doors to unlock and push.*

Picture a vision. Imagine the comfort—and coolness—it will bring to the eyes of our loved ones. Keeping the big picture in mind will give us the strength to impact others, especially our loved ones.

'Ā'ishah ﷺ is a prime example of someone who challenged herself to learn something new. She was an expert in Qur'an, hadith, legal rulings, poetry, genealogy, history, and had expanded her knowledge of medicine. The nephew of 'Ā'ishah ﷺ, 'Urwah ibn Zubayr ﷺ, once asked her where she attained her knowledge of medicine.

'Ā'ishah ﷺ said that the Prophet ﷺ fell ill towards the end of his life, and people would make prescriptions based on the medicine from their hometowns. This was how she learned the proper treatments for different ailments.

'Ā'ishah ﷺ actively learned how to best care for the Prophet ﷺ. She was not afraid to push her limits with something new. *She was not afraid to unlock and push doors open.*

She helped others based on whatever she learned. She raised orphaned girls into scholars. One such girl was 'Ā'ishah bint Ṭalḥah ﷺ, who became a jurist. 'Ā'ishah bint Ṭalḥah ﷺ asked 'Ā'ishah ﷺ what to do with the letters that were sent with gifts that she received from strangers. 'Ā'ishah ﷺ encouraged her student to not only reply, but to also reply with gifts.[15] A'ishah ﷺ encouraged a life of service. The drive of being there for others for the sake of Allah ﷻ was, therefore, a tremendous driving force. People accused her of things that she did not do, but that did not stop her from giving back to the community. Her love of Allah ﷻ and wanting to be there for His creation were greater.

---

15 Shaykh Akram Nadwi, Diploma in Islamic Female Scholarship Week 3 recording, Cambridge Islamic College

We may get discriminated against for our circumstances. Still, that stigma should not stop us from succeeding for our loved ones. Excelling in our field is a way to do good towards those we love.

Allah ﷻ promises,

> *'Allah does not leave to waste the reward of the doers of good.'*
> (*Yūsuf* 12: 90)

5. Silence the Noise from Those That Try to Cage You.

Some people will pull us down as we grow; put us in a box so our petals will not bloom. Take in constructive criticism but do not take destructive criticism. Daisy was criticizing me for doing a talk and not updating her that I would. This was destructive criticism. There was no room for growth from her reaction. There was only the harm of being demeaned. The harm of being treated as though I were undeserving of growth or success.

No one deserves to be caged.

Everyone is worthy of unlocking their potential.

Everyone is worthy of the bloom.

6. Continuously Purify Your Heart and Go Back to Your Vision.

It is easy to feel shaken when we are caged. It is hurtful to be pushed into a position where we are forced to exclaim that we deserve to be treated like everyone else. This could blur our vision because we are consumed with the pain of not just pushing our petals out to bloom, but we are also clinging to the ground to demonstrate that we belong.

Let go of that hurt despite the pain flooding through. Let us top pushing, or clinging, and remind ourselves of our vision. Remind ourselves of the good we want to do. People might push us, but it does not mean we must prove that we belong. We must refocus on our goal and vision as if we did not come across stigmatized judgement. Cleanse ourselves from that toxic exposure. Purify our hearts and souls.

Do this by staying away from such environments and turning to Allah ﷻ. Asking Him to give us continuous strength will help us continue to be who we are: a soul that wants to grow and do good towards others, for the love of Allah ﷻ.

The story of Prophet Ibrāhīm ﷺ is about discovering and unlocking our potential with a pure heart.

The people of Ibrāhīm ﷺ worshipped idols. Through deductive reasoning, he discovered that idols should not be worshipped. He went in pursuit of the One deserving of worship. He traveled—took the action of discovering—and met people who worshipped the sun, the stars, and the moon. He genuinely tried to discover the Creator—his Creator. He concluded that God is the Creator of all things and is beyond this universe. It is through sincerely finding God—through deductive reasoning and actively searching—that Ibrāhīm ﷺ found his purpose.

> *'And one who followed his way was Ibrāhīm when **he approached his Lord with a pure heart.**'*
>
> (al-Ṣāffāt 37: 83–4)

Approach life with a pure heart, because when we do, we will discover and unlock our potential in a blessed manner no matter the number of times people try to cage us.

Prophet Ibrāhīm ﷺ had to leave his wife Hājar ﷺ and his baby Ismā'īl ﷺ at a barren land—Makkah—where there was no potential for water, let alone growth of life. Hājar ﷺ ran back and forth in pursuit of water or any sign of life. Eventually, the water of Zamzam gushed forth. A land thought barren—without potential—had the potential of life all along. It was considered impossible, but there is always that potential for bloom.

Let us hold on to our vision and keep trying to achieve our goals. Keeping our loved ones as our driving force will facilitate our potential to gush forth.

Travelers who noticed the spring of Zamzam asked Hājar ﷺ if they could settle in Makkah. Her driving force of finding sustenance for her son turned a barren land that was once empty into a community of growth. Ibrāhīm ﷺ later returned and built what will become the most central and sacred structure in Islam— the Kaaba, the House of Allah.

Why was that barren land chosen to house the Kaaba? It is a reminder for us to believe.

Everything and every one of us is worthy of unleashing and unlocking our potential free.

Chapter 9

From Inspirational Figures of the Past to the Blooming You of Tomorrow

My husband was previously an atheist and thought that religions were mainly scriptures—with a bunch of stories on figures of the past—about delusional hope. He considered this hope harmful when facing life's realities. He later embraced Islam after coming across the book *The Qur'an and Science,* which included verses on the creation and the ending of the universe, which aligned with what he read on the Big Bang theory and Crunch theory. He could later see from my public written work that the stories of the Prophets helped me cope with life's realities. *It was not delusional hope.* It was a practical and rationalized hope that put life in perspective.

Brené Brown says in her book, *The Gifts of Imperfections*, that perspective through hope helps:

'to develop understanding and move forward.'[16]

Stories of the Prophets are, therefore, a guide for us to grow.

We are meant to gain inspiration from the legacies of the Prophets and those who followed their examples so that we may bloom tomorrow.

We are all planted in this world and have something to give.

The only aspect that distinguishes us is how we release that strength from within. We need to choose whether to complain with defeat or believe that we can bloom. We need to give ourselves the chance to face and accept reality for what it is instead of being in denial just to avoid the gloom. We need to be amongst those who embrace our innate nature by allowing ourselves to process grief. We need to decide whether to remain entrapped with anxiety or push through that fear.

Will we answer our call to courage?

Do we hear His call through the Prophets?

Prophets also experienced fear and grief and called out to the Lord of the worlds about it.

We may feel guilty for the time we have lost in not answering that call, but we can shed that guilt through repentance. We can

---

16 (Brown 2010, 74)

rectify our mistakes and display that effort to move forward. This effort can be shown by being the better version of ourselves. Strive to become the version that does not dwell in guilt or sorrow.

We may go through that cycle of repeatedly letting go of pain to forgive. There is no harm in finally shutting that door. Walk away from those who regularly harm you to break free. Consult the sincere to see the picture more clearly. We are meant to value our worth so that we find the strength to step into the world.

Are you ready to rise from the ground and display the essence of your core?

We are not meant to remain guarded. Our humanity is meant to be let out. Put down your mask and reveal your true authentic self. Our vulnerable selves can shake society into growth. *Find strength from warriors sent by God.* Let their kindness give strength to your rise. This is how we can remain rooted without any need for disguises.

We might face those who have the potential to drag us down. We might be pushed into defeat. Remember that those who bury us just do not want us to take that leap. They do not want us to leap in unleashing our gifts out in the world. They prefer that we remain caged and buried beneath the ground. Allow the sincere to lift you. Honour them with this gift. Never forget to trust your instincts and be sure to voice them out.

Those who lift others will show us how we have a destined purpose. They will remind us of our strengths. This is when we should redirect ourselves to our vision and purify our intentions. Refocus on your goals—march towards your vision with hope.

Those before us succeeded with grace. They did not treat anyone as insignificant and weak. Allah ﷻ preserved their legacies for us to reflect upon. He even told us how Prophet Sulaymān ﷺ stopped his army to let ants pass. He showed us what makes an army strong, and that is by caring for every living thing. We are planted in this world not to be uprooted by life's winds; we are meant to rise and bloom with grace.

We are destined to unleash that strength from within.

The Near end of this Climb—the Planting of my Seed

I was near the end of reaching my climb in completing this book—with just a few more chapters to write—when I got sick. This affected my writing schedule. It was not the flu nor the fever that frustrated me, but the cough that would not go away. It was so hard to breathe without the breathing machine that I had to remain lying down most of the time. Medicines were not effective, and it was painful to lift my phone for long to type. I could not turn my mind off either, so I continued to jot down notes for this last chapter. I had the ending in mind—planting an overall message—but I did not know the last few steps to plant the seed effectively. It was frustrating because I was at the peak, with the seed ready to sow, but I could not seem to plant it no matter how hard I tried.

I struggled to inhale, despite using the machine, and I felt pressed into defeat.

'What was I thinking, promising to write a book—I cannot even cough properly.'

I recalled what my eight-year-old self had promised at the hospital. I was recovering from pneumonia, with one of my lungs previously collapsing. My chest was hurting like it was now, and I was confined to the bed. I was in a more severe state then, and at twenty-seven years, I could not fathom what the eight-year-old me had been thinking. Why had I made such a promise to get out of the hospital? It is difficult to do anything with my health, so why have this big dream, and make hard promises? Why write a book on strength when I am clearly physically weak and will always be struggling to let out strength from within? It will always be difficult; why make my life harder? *With only a few chapters left to complete the book, I thought this was the worst possible time to get sick.* I could not understand what had propelled me to make that difficult promise as a child.

This was when I fumbled for my phone, and on Instagram, I found a post that answered my whys. It was about baby Maryam, who is a child with Spinal Muscular Atrophy. Her parents were trying to raise petition signatures for the government to approve a drug treatment that could be a cure. I remembered knowing another child—my dearest friend Iman—with the same illness. I got to know her when she was six. She is now ten years old, blooming in the most beautiful of ways. Her mother sent me a video of Iman giving a speech on raising awareness for SMA. I beamed, watching her rise. I cannot wait to see the ways she will bloom tomorrow. I messaged baby Maryam's parents with prayers and told them of Iman. I hoped that they would find comfort in being in touch with parents who have children going through the same or similar diagnoses. It was when I sent that message that I realized: this was the answer to my question. This was why I had been propelled to make that promise as a child.

I promised as a child that I would write a book inspired by the stories of the Prophets based on my life with disabilities. I prayed that it would be a means to encourage and give hope to everyone, especially those going through hardships. I hoped that it could be a way to be there for hospitalized children like me and for parents like my parents. A way to take away the pain and reassure them of their inner strength. A way to feel grateful for being alive. I promised that I would share the process of my climb based on being inspired by the stories of the Prophets so that others can recognize that they can make the climb as well.

Below I have written a piece summarizing my climb on the journey of this book. This poetic-prose completes the fulfillment of my promise, and with it, I pray we can all bloom together.

The pain that your body endures, from muscle spasms to the weakness of your knees. The stumbles and falls. The rods needed to make sure that you continued to stand, and the stitches to make sure that you would not bleed. The battle of the mind that follows, from the confusion of why life was hard. The questioning if you were getting weaker, and why you have to put in effort simply for being born.

*Denials over life's harsh reality emerge. The whys and hows. You want to be let out. You only see darkness and feel like you are buried beneath the ground. You cannot move and find it hard to breathe. You are forced to see how trials are part of life's reality. Time passes by without a change of tide. You are pushed to accept and comply. Life is meant to be this way. **You have no choice but to endure the hardships you face.** Life's trials are real. It is part of growth. Anxiety engulfs, and fear soon follows. You hurl to your knees and prefer to wallow. You squirm for the end to be near. How to push through, stay strong, and face difficulties without fear.*

You crumble before you begin.

Life passes by that you start to feel guilt. You recall the promise you made that you must fulfill. The potential that you have inside. Why give up before you try? You try to muster up the strength instead of hide. You look beyond your life and circumstances. You remember the stories of the Prophets and how they made the climb. You push yourself up with the help of those who are kind. Those who are sincere and were always there. Those who believe in you and hold you dear. You make your way but only to be faced with spears. Spears from other people that are not sincere. People who carelessly harm. They hurt you, and you get alarmed. **Why did they behave this way?** *Why do I have to remove arrows from my chest? How do I protect myself?* **I must choose to be guarded.**

You try to forgive and let go of the pain. You know that this is the only way. The way to move forward without revenge. Anger is not meant to be kept. You gain strength from forgiving and letting go. Pain that you do not want to hold close. You battle with fear of having to go through harm again. You start to carry this armour instead. It might protect you from getting hurt. You climb up but only to lose a part of yourself. You being guarded means hiding behind steel. A way for you to conceal a part of what is real. A piece of who you are. **You believe that you should have been guarded from the start.** *This is the only way to survive. It keeps you strong when following the tide. It safeguards your heart from having to break. You start to be part of the crowd but without being fully awake.*

Guardedness was, in reality, preventing your humanity from coming out. The wholeness of your humanity and the essence of your soul. The vulnerabilities inside and what makes you whole. You recognize that letting your guard down is true strength. You must embrace being your whole self again. Wholehearted living is a life that you now want to abide. You hold on firmly to the belief that kindness saves lives. You take your armour off even though you wrestle with fear. Again, you notice the sincere. **Warriors sent by God.** *Souls like you. Those who strive to protect others from getting bruised. Their priority is not just to survive. They have a bigger purpose in life.*

You narrate with words because that is the door you can unlock and push. Words your grandfather promised that you one day could. You uncaged yourself and let that unlocked potential burst. **Everyone has potential, just like their hearts.** *You still try to show up fully when off-stage even though people try to cage. You find yourself cast away, looked down, and mocked. Peers who do not fail to remind you that you do not belong.*

'Why are you even here? Shouldn't you be at home?'

They cannot stand the sight of you for showing up whole.

You remember how people tried to control your life. The hurdles they placed so that you do not climb. You still carry the seed in your hand. It was meant to be planted. You promised God, you planned. Your loved ones remind you of your strength. How these hurdles may be big, but Allah strengthens the weak. He tests them in different ways for them to take the leap. Find their courage and strength inside. The oppressed always eventually rise. You just need to march forth and keep moving on. Stand firmly on your feet, and stay strong.

The ground beneath you shakes.

Allah keeps testing you in different ways.

You are told that you have been standing and walking wrong. Your physiotherapist teaches you a new way to explore. You are not sure if this is what your muscles can take. Why is restarting from scratch always your fate? **You do not know how long you can do this.** *How much left is there of the climb? The slope is too steep. You are unsure if you can plant on time. You are close to the finish that you just need to make that last stride. You walk with your family, but soon you have to try. Try to make these last few steps on your own. Plant the seed and water it with what you know.*

You trust that your roots are firmly in place. The stories of the Prophets have paved a way. Allah poured the light for your seed to take. You are near the next stage. You start to see a slight of green emerge. The sprout from your seed is ready to burst. You smile and cultivate with thirst. You are beginning to understand Allah's plans. How Allah's promises are true, so be glad. You are placed in hardship so that you grow. He does not abandon any soul.

Look at the inspirational blooming figures of the past for the blooming you of tomorrow. *This is a way to grow on a land barren and cracked without sorrow. The legacies of the Prophets are meant to help you grow, so you may bloom before you go Home. Each chapter and line is a means to discover your strength. A way to plant and flourish with belief. Shine even when people say no. Your yellow petals are meant to burst and glow. Burst with life. Burst with joy. Burst to lift others instead of cry. Your petals may fall out of hurt, but that does not mean you give up. You are firmly planted. You belong. You are meant to make a change. Stand strong.*

There is potential in every soul.

Your bloom for tomorrow is waiting for you to face, because you are meant to embrace.

Embrace and leave behind.

A legacy.

A mark.

An encouragement to climb.

A legacy to leave, so that you may unite with those from history. The Prophets and Companions who were pure from the core. Those who followed their footsteps and moved as a whole. Moved towards compassion, kindness, and growth. Moved towards building bridges instead of walls. They were warriors but without armour or shields. They spoke with kindness even if their hearts grieved. They knew that their tests were just paving a way, so that we may all one day meet Allah after having bloomed, and collectively say...

'O Allah...Your promise was true.'

Announcement of Upcoming Book

RISE WITH GRACE

Personal insights on healing from stigma and cultivating our communities based on my life with physical disabilities.

'Rise with Grace' will be more centered on the disability experience within the community, especially as a Muslim. The hardships within the community are considered the most challenging within the disability experience. Three of the chapters were originally written for 'Strength from Within' but there would be more room to propose solutions with a second book. This second book will delve into the stereotypes, marginalization, and stigmas faced, and the impact they can have on people with disabilities and their families. It will be a book on healing and a call of courage for them to live out their lives, especially out of wanting to follow the way of the Prophets and Islamic legacies before us. It will also be a call of courage to community leaders and community members to rise with grace in building a more inclusive, understanding, and accommodating society based on the Prophetic example of leadership.

'Rise with Grace' intends to be a deep-dive into the intersection of disability & Islam, so that readers from diverse backgrounds can learn about both the disability lived experience and the Islamic framework of community care towards people with disabilities and their families.

Readers' Discussion Circle on Book 'Strength from Within'

Discuss to collectively rise and bloom

Preface

1. What are the benefits of turning to Allah ﷻ instead of people?
2. What are the potential benefits of book-reading when going through a difficulty?
3. What are the benefits of reading the stories of the Prophets?

Chapter 1: Trials in Life—A Seed Preparing to Sprout

1. What is the reality of this life?
2. What attitudes must one avoid when interacting with a child going through a trial?
3. What is the purpose of life's trials?
4. What are the qualities of those who accept trials?

5. How do we shift from destructive questioning to constructive questioning?
6. How to strengthen those hospitalized when visiting them?

Chapter 2: The Process of Accepting Life's Trials

1. Describe our nature as human beings.
2. How to practice acceptance towards life's trials?
3. What can we learn from the story of Ādam ﷺ with regards to processing grief and accepting life's reality?
4. What are the harms of escapism and denial?
5. What is the healthiest way to complain?
6. How do we help children process and accept life's trials?
7. What is our purpose on this Earth as believers?
8. How is vulnerability strength?

Chapter 3: Entrapment due to Anxieties

1. What are the anxieties those with invincible disabilities can face?
2. What is a possible source of our anxieties?
3. What can we shift in mindset to release ourselves from anxiety?
4. List out actions that we can do to tackle anxiety.
5. What does Islam say on marriage for those with disabilities?
6. How can family members help one deal with anxiety?
7. List out what Allah ﷻ expects from us versus what Satan expects from us.
8. What can we learn from the story of Ayyūb ﷺ when dealing with distress?
9. What can we learn from the story of Yūnus ﷺ when dealing with anxiety?
10. What is the purpose of remembering Allah's Names?

Chapter 4: From Fear to Courage

1. What is courage?
2. How can we face our fears as believers?
3. What does the story of Mūsā ﷺ teach us when it comes to facing our fears?
4. What can be our call to courage?

Chapter 5: From Guilt to Forgiveness of the Self

1. What is the difference between shame and guilt?
2. What are the benefits of guilt?
3. What are the harms of not forgiving ourselves?
4. What are the fears those with disabilities face when interacting with their siblings?
5. What are the fears that siblings of those with disabilities face?
6. How should we behave with family members when going through a trial?
7. What can we learn from the story of Yūnus ﷺ on forgiving ourselves?
8. What are the steps towards self-forgiveness?

Chapter 6: From Holder of Pain to Forgiver of Others

1. What is the reality those with disabilities can potentially face with people?
2. What is 'ableism' and what are some examples of ableism?
3. How can productivity help one let go of pain and forgive?
4. What is 'gaslighting' and what are its harms?
5. What are the fruits of forgiveness?
6. What are the steps to make it easier to let go of pain and forgive?

7. What can we learn through the examples of Ya'qūb ﷺ and Yūsuf ﷺ on forgiveness?
8. What may be some reasons people inflict pain?
9. What is the significance behind the prayer of the oppressed?
10. What are the harms of overly zooming in on the positive?
11. What are the steps towards healing from pain?

Chapter 7: From Guarded to Approachable

1. Why may one be guarded?
2. What are the harms or the potential losses incurred from remaining guarded?
3. How can boundaries help us remain both unguarded and approachable?
4. How to establish healthy boundaries?
5. What are the fruits of being wholeheartedly present?
6. How should we select our friends?
7. What are the qualities of a 'warrior sent by God'?

Chapter 8: From Caged-in to Unlocking Potential

1. How was Prophet Muhammad ﷺ with all children and how should that shape us as adults?
2. What are the fruits of sharing experiences?
3. How has Allah ﷻ arranged plans for those with disabilities?
4. What are the benefits of internalizing our experiences?
5. What are the benefits of befriending those with disabilities?
6. How does Allah ﷻ help us discover our gifts?
7. List out the signs that Allah ﷻ has revealed in your 'lift'.
8. How does Allah ﷻ help us throughout our journey of growth?
9. What are the gifts of 'hearing' and sight' Allah has given us?
10. How to strengthen our hope?

11. Who are the 'owners of strength' as described in the Qur'an?
12. Give examples of constructive criticism and destructive criticism.
13. What can we learn from the story of Ibrāhīm ﷺ when it comes to discovering our potential?

Chapter 9: From Inspirational Figures of the Past to the Blooming You of Tomorrow

1. How can the stories of the Prophets help us rationalize hope?
2. What is the promise of Allah ﷻ?
3. List out ways you hope to bloom.

Bibliography

Brown, Brené. *The Gifts of Imperfections*. Simon & Schuster, 2010

Brown, Brené. *Rising Strong*. Spiegel & Grau, 2015

Ibn Kathir, *Stories of the Prophets*. Darussalam, 2014

Ibn Tayimiyyah, *Gardens of Purification*. Dar As-Sunnah Publishers, 2016

Shaykh Akram Nadwi, *Diploma in Islamic Female Scholarship Week 3 recording*, Cambridge Islamic College

Qur'an translation: www.quran.com Sahih international translation

Hadith:
1. Muslim, Ṣifat al-Munāfiqīn, 58
2. Abū Dāwūd, Book of General Behaviour, 169
3. Tirmidhī, Chapters on Righteousness and Maintaining Good Relations with Relatives, 120
4. Ṣaḥīḥ al-Bukhārī, Book of Sales and Trade, 2072
5. Ṣaḥīḥ al-Bukhārī, The Book of Miscellany, 642
6. Musnad Aḥmed, Musnad al-Mukatharin, 12286